ALLIED AIRCRAFT OF

A PHOTOGRAPHIC GUIDE TO THE SURVIVING AIRCRAFT OF THE NORMANDY LANDINGS

LEE CHAPMAN

For Dad, Keith Alan Chapman, 1951–2020

Author's Note

The author has tried to document as many of the surviving D-Day aircraft as possible, and whilst it was not possible to photograph every type (especially during a global pandemic), this book seeks to provide examples of as many aircraft types that played a significant role in the weeks surrounding the Normandy invasion. The book deliberately includes a small number of supporting aircraft, which, whilst not participants on D-Day itself, were an indispensable part of the Allied effort that enabled a successful invasion.

Within this book the term 'D-Day aircraft' has been used to refer to any aircraft involved in the preparation, planning and follow-up stages surrounding 6 June 1944, as well as those directly involved on the day itself. Occasionally, the author has also included later or alternative marks of aircraft that were not active during 1944, to demonstrate where similar types can be seen today. Sadly, some significant aircraft types have not survived the test of time. As this is a guide to modern-day survivors, these extinct aircraft types have not been included in this book. This is not a reflection on their involvement during the operations.

Finally, classifying aircraft in use during 1944 is a minefield. Most aircraft would be classified into what we now call 'multi-role' aircraft, whereby they would be used for a range of purposes. To further confuse the matter, some aircraft were designed with one intention but adapted to another purpose as the war progressed and technology moved on. For this book, the author has attempted to include aircraft within the section that most clearly defines its D-Day activities; some aircraft types appear in more than one chapter where there is a specific story to tell.

Published by Key Books
An imprint of Key Publishing Ltd
PO Box 100
Stamford
Lincs PE19 1XQ

www.keypublishing.com

The right of Lee Chapman to be identified as the author of this book has been asserted in accordance with the Copyright, Designs and Patents Act 1988 Sections 77 and 78.

ISBN 978 1 913870 40 9

Typeset by SJmagic DESIGN SERVICES, India.

CONTENTS

FOREWORD

Ever since I was a little boy, I have always thought of the DC-3 as an iconic aeroplane. At that point in time, however, I wouldn't have even known the difference between a DC-3 and a C-47. It is only since having had the privilege of flying, owning and restoring one, that I have really begun to understand and appreciate its true importance.

C-47, DC-3, Dakota, Dak, Gooney Bird, call it what you will; an aircraft built in the 1930s that is still flying today is testament to a truly magnificent design. It's somewhat ironic that an aircraft designed to carry passengers was perhaps one of the pieces of equipment hailed as turning the tide of the Second World War. To quote Dwight. D. Eisenhower, "Four other pieces of equipment that most senior officers came to regard as among the most vital to our success in Africa and Europe were the bulldozer, the jeep, the 2-ton truck, and the C-47 airplane." Curiously, none of these were designed for combat.

Not only did the aircraft turn the tide of the war, it also went on to start commercial aviation as we know it today. I think it's arguably the most successful aircraft design of all time.

Flying a C-47 or a DC-3 is a unique privilege. One I think that pilots across the world would jump at, given the chance. It's a relatively simple aeroplane in terms of its design and systems, but it can certainly be a handful on the ground and in the critical phases of flight. Nothing can beat the sound of the twin Pratt & Whitney Wasps firing into life; it's a sound that resonates with aviation enthusiasts everywhere.

I am incredibly honoured to be not only the pilot for *Night Fright* but also the owner and project leader of the *Night Fright* C-47 Restoration Project. I see myself as a custodian of a piece of history, and it's my job to preserve it and inspire the future generation of historians, aviators and engineers. The project has taught me just what an incredible piece of engineering the C-47 is, its importance to the war effort and the unwavering courage of the men who flew from them and jumped out of them.

Much has been written and will be written about D-Day. Most people associate D-Day with the seaborne invasion. Whilst that is of course true, I, however, think of C-47s, paratroopers and gliders. It's barely imaginable what those men would have gone through, sitting unarmed in the back of C-47s and gliders awaiting their fate. I think there has been a perception that the C-47 was just a 'transport aircraft'. It's not until more recently that people have begun to see them as true warbirds, which of course they are. Since the 75th anniversary of D-Day in 2019, there has been a greater appreciation of the C-47 and its importance. This is something that will only continue as time passes. I couldn't be prouder to be restoring *Night Fright* to her 1944 configuration as a flying memorial to those who fought for our freedom.

Charlie Walker
Owner and pilot of C-47 *Night Fright*

PREFACE

Operation *Overlord*, the Allied invasion of France in 1944, is possibly the most widely discussed event of the Second World War. It was the turning point in the conflict; the moment when the Allies took the fight to the enemy which ultimately led to victory. The aircraft that supported the invasion have become legendary; Spitfires, Mosquitos, Mustangs and Dakotas have all earned their place in history for their deeds during the Second World War. This book explores the roles that these and many other aircraft played during the Allied invasion.

The year 1944 saw great leaps in aviation technology. New aircraft arrived at the front line with better armament, fire power, speed, altitude and range. The coming together of the Allied forces brought the might of the Royal Air Force and its commonwealth Allies together with the seemingly infinite resources of the USAAF. The result was an eclectic force of wooden gliders, heavy bombers, agile fighters, powerful ground attack, rugged transport and light liaison aircraft.

This book features a potted history of many of the Allied aircraft that were involved in the operations surrounding the Normandy invasion. It includes details of the aircraft that flew reconnaissance missions, ground attack and early bombing raids that cleared the path for the invasion. The book will also include the aircraft that flew on D-Day itself, including the decoys, fighter escorts and the troop and equipment transportation aircraft. The story will be told using high-quality images of surviving and restored aircraft in the air, on the ground and within our museums.

The images have been drawn from the author's personal collection. As a media photographer and keen enthusiast, he has attended many airshows, flypasts and museum events over the last ten years. He has been fortunate to get up close and photograph aircraft representative of many of the surviving types used during the period. Many of the images to feature in the book will also include airframes with genuine D-Day experience; there are many surviving aircraft with fascinating stories to tell. Where genuine aircraft were not available, similar marks or representative types have been used to complete the story.

Acknowledgements

The author and publisher would like to thank the following organisations for permission to use copyright material in this book: the Shuttleworth Collection, the Avro Heritage Museum, the de Havilland Aircraft Museum, the Army Flying Museum, East Kirkby Aviation Museum, the Imperial War Museum and the RAF Museum for permissions to photograph their exhibits on their sites. Every attempt has been made to seek permissions for copyright material and photographic rights in this book. However, if we have inadvertently used materials without permission, we apologise, and we will make the necessary correction at the first opportunity.

The author would also like to thank Georgia Massey for all her support and patience, Andy 'Loopy' Forester and Daniel Gooch for joining him on aircraft photography adventures. He would also like to acknowledge the support given to him from Charlie Walker of the *Night Fright* Restoration Project. The author would also like to credit Ian Grigg for his support and for many of the photographic opportunities that he has helped to provide through Airscene. Finally, the author would like to acknowledge the hard work of airshow organisers, warbird operators, restorers, conservators and museum curators that keep the memories alive.

CHAPTER 1

INTRODUCTION

A Douglas C-47 Skytrain prepares to leave for France with a full complement of paratroopers on board.

Two P-51 Mustangs, one in RAF colours and the other in USAAF colours, fly together representing the combined Allied air forces, which became known as the Allied Expeditionary Air Force (AEAF).

Operation *Overlord* was the codename given to the Allied invasion of German-occupied Northern France. Almost 160,000 troops landed on the Normandy beaches in just one day; this was the largest military operation in history. The huge land-based force also required unprecedented support from both naval and aerial elements. The Royal Air Force (RAF) and United States Army Air Forces (USAAF) provided troop transport, air cover, bombing and ground attack, as well as key information through photographic reconnaissance missions.

On 15 November 1943, the Allied Expeditionary Air Force (AEAF) was formed under the command of Air Marshal Sir Trafford Leigh-Mallory. This brought together resources from the RAF (including its commonwealth Allies), the Tactical Air Force and the Ninth US Air Force into one unit ready for Operation *Overlord*. General Eisenhower was appointed as the Supreme Allied commander overseeing all the forces. Air Chief Marshal Sir Arthur Tedder was appointed as the deputy and retained many aspects of control over the AEAF, which often made decision making complex.

Although the 6 June 1944, D-Day, is remembered above all others, the preparations for the Allied invasion of France were under discussion for over a year prior to that date. From February 1944, the range of aerial activity over northern Europe intensified, in preparation for the beginning of the invasion proper. The first stage was reconnaissance, where high-altitude photographic missions would be flown to locate suitable landing locations and to pinpoint enemy defences. A period of heavy bombing and ground-attack missions followed, along with fighter sweeps to ensure that the Allies had control of the skies.

The famous paratrooper dropping missions (as recreated here on the 75th anniversary *Daks over Normandy* event), which are now synonymous with D-Day, were only part of the story. On D-Day itself around 12,000 aircraft were involved, flying almost 15,000 sorties. Only 127 of these aircraft were lost, a testament to the success of the earlier raids that had largely cleared the skies of the Luftwaffe and destroyed German radar stations and anti-aircraft batteries.

The Battle of Britain Memorial Flight's (BBMF) Douglas Dakota (ZA947) demonstrates the 'invasion stripe' look.

The Allied invasion was a multinational affair, with massive contributions from most of the free world. Most significantly, the British, American and Canadian forces joined together to mount a massive aerial armada. The sheer number of Allied aircraft in the skies meant that aeroplanes were far more likely to be shot down by friendly fire than a German aircraft. It was therefore deemed necessary to ensure that all Allied aircraft were easily identifiable. A few days before the event, the order was given to mark all aircraft with the standardised five alternating black and white 'invasion stripes' on both wings and the fuselage.

Due to the very short notice and the scale of the task, most of the stripes were hastily applied by groundcrew with limited resources; as such, many of the stripes were far from neat and tidy. One month after D-Day, the stripes were removed from the upper surfaces of planes based in France to ensure they were better camouflaged on the ground. By the end of 1944, air supremacy was so great that the stripes were no longer required and therefore completely removed from all aircraft. Today, many surviving aircraft wear the stripes in honour of those who took part in the historic Allied invasion.

In the months leading up to D-Day, squadrons of Hawker Typhoons and Supermarine Spitfires were sent on intense ground-attack missions to target radar installations. Meanwhile, Avro Lancaster, Short Stirling and Handley Page Halifax bombers were tasked with the destruction of wireless and listening stations. It was also important to ensure that bombing did not focus purely on one area that would highlight to the enemy where the invasion would take place. Even on D-Day itself, diversionary tactics were employed: the famous 617 *Dambusters* Squadron dropped small metal strips know as 'chaff' over the Pas-de-Calais region to confuse the few remaining German radar stations.

The BBMF's Avro Lancaster is currently one of only two airworthy Lancasters in the world. The other aircraft is based in Canada, but a long-term project in the UK could see a third Lancaster flying in the next few years. Often heavy bombers would be escorted into bombing missions with fighter aircraft such as the Supermarine Spitfire, as seen here. The BBMF also operate several fighter aircraft including this Spitfire which, although a later variant, is given the markings of a D-Day reconnaissance aircraft. The red nose spinner was borrowed from another aircraft for this flight; it would have been blue during the 1944 operations.

The vast resources of America and Canada provided immeasurable support to the British war effort. Not only did both nations send their own troops and machinery in unprecedented numbers, but both countries were also able to support in supplies of equipment directly to the British forces as well as equipping their own squadrons. Large numbers of British-designed aircraft were built in Canada, and American aircraft designs such as the North American Mustang were not only operated by the USAAF but also the RAF.

The North American Mustang was a triumph in international co-operation. It married the North American airframe with the world-beating Rolls-Royce designed British Merlin engine, which was also built under licence in America by Packard. The aircraft was a huge success, capable of flying into Germany and back on a single mission. It operated for the RAF and USAAF in large numbers, examples of markings from both air forces are visible in this image.

The USAAF operated from bases in the south of England. The 6th Airborne Division aimed for the Caen area of France, whilst the US 82nd and 101st Airborne Divisions were dropped south of the Cotentin Peninsula. Their aim was to secure the flanks and prevent a German counter-attack on the beaches. Almost 800 C-47 Skytrains towing over 300 Hadrian and Horsa gliders took the troops to the fight. The drops were not as accurate as hoped. Thick cloud and heavy flak caused the formations to break up, resulting in the scattering of troops away from the intended drop zones. Of the 6,600 soldiers that headed for Sainte-Mère-Église, only 1,100 landed near their objective.

Douglas C-47 41-18401 is painted as a tribute to the 101st Airborne Division who were dropped into France on 6 June 1944. Built in 1942, 41-18401 was taken into military service but never actually allocated to an operational squadron. The aeroplane was eventually handed over to Pan American airlines for civilian service but now appears as a typical C-47 would have done in June 1944.

The British 6th Airborne Division, commanded by Major General Richard 'Windy' Gale, was tasked with capturing key strategic targets behind enemy lines. This included the now famous Pegasus Bridge. Six Halifax bombers towing Airspeed Horsa gliders containing the men of 'D' Company took off just before 11pm on 5 June 1944. In a remarkable piece of flying, the gliders landed successful in-between the two target bridges and were able to capture them in little over ten minutes.

The Army Flying Museum in Hampshire hosts an impressive collection of assault gliders, including this Airspeed Horsa Mk II. Due to their wooden structure and disposable nature, very few original D-Day gliders remain; they were often built with the intention of using them only once. Mechanisms were fitted to some of the glider-tug aircraft in an attempt to recover them from northern France, but this was a tricky operation and not always worth the risk.

A selection of Allied fighters lined up at Duxford: P47 Thunderbolt, two Spitfires and a Grumman Wildcat. A post-war Bearcat is also just visible in this image.

During the planning stages of the Normandy invasions, three conditions were identified as essential to success: firstly, the Allies must have air superiority to ensure that enemy aircraft could not hamper landing plans. Secondly, an element of surprise must be maintained, and finally, the enemy must not be able to build up sufficient defences to counter any attacks.

The AEAF had many roles to play in the build-up to Operation *Overlord* to ensure these conditions were met. Fighters and light bombers would be required to sweep the areas and destroy the Luftwaffe both on the ground and in the air. Factories and railways were also heavily targeted to ensure that the Germans could not resupply the lines. These pre-invasion attacks proved so successful that on D-Day, casualties and losses were only 25 per cent of what was anticipated.

A Boeing B-17 is accompanied by two Douglas C-47s.

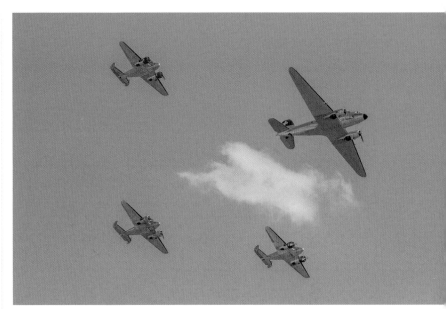

Three Beech-18s and a DC-3 of the Swiss Classic Formation represent some of the transport aircraft types in service in 1944. Many of these aircraft would be adapted for civilian use and pioneer the air travel industry after the war.

The aerial operation on 6 June 1944 was a momentous undertaking, but was only a small part of the mind-blowing logistics involved in Operation *Overlord* as a whole. Although the pre-invasion raids had successfully neutralised many of the German defences, there was still considerable opposition to be overcome. Success was far from guaranteed; several different aircraft types were involved in a multitude of different roles both on D-Day itself and in the weeks surrounding the invasion. Success of the invasion and many lives depended on the AEAF's ability to clear the path.

This book can only attempt to capture a small element of the aerial activity over France in the spring of 1944. Although many aircraft types did not make it, we are fortunate that a booming warbird industry and huge preservation scene has kept many of these aircraft alive for us to see today. The sheer variety of aircraft types reflects the rapid technological advancements of war and the complex nature of the task at hand.

CHAPTER 2

RECONNAISSANCE AIRCRAFT

Two Supermarine Spitfire PR Mk XI aircraft photographed at Old Warden airfield.

A typical camera used during the period sits in front of a PR Mk XI Spitfire.

The original Normandy briefing boards can be seen in the Airborne Assault Museum at Duxford.

After the disastrous attempt to land an invasion force at Dieppe, France in 1942, the Allies were keen to avoid another catastrophe. To ensure nothing was left to chance, a huge undertaking of intelligence gathering was required. The French Resistance and a few very dangerous covert landing missions were able to provide some intelligence, but most of the information came from aerial photography. Dangerous missions, often by lone, unarmed aircraft deep behind enemy lines were undertaken to obtain precious photographic data.

From 1942, the RAF's 140 Squadron was tasked with gathering the photographs. Initially, specially adapted photo-reconnaissance Supermarine Spitfires were fitted with a range of large cameras and extra fuel tanks. Weapons were also removed to enhance speed, altitude and range. Careful flight planning using a slight overlap could produce stereoscopic images which could give an indication of height and depth of the landscape. When combined with tide times and other data, the images could be converted into accurate three-dimensional representations of the area, which proved a vital aid to planning.

Photo-reconnaissance pilots and crew had a busy workload in the 18-month build-up to the invasion. Firstly, a suitable location for the invasion had to be found, which meant surveying vast areas across the German front line. Pilots were sent on missions to scout out suitable landing beaches with limited military defences. Missions were also undertaken around these areas to locate German airfields, radar stations, factories and railways so that these could be destroyed prior to the invasion. Once Normandy was confirmed as a suitable location, photographic reconnaissance flights continued across the whole of northern France to ensure that no clues of the invasion location would be given to the enemy.

The Spitfire PR Mk XI was the most numerous photo-reconnaissance aircraft in use during the period. It entered service during the summer of 1943 and was either painted in the iconic PR blue colour or light pink in order to avoid detection on its high-altitude missions. Two Spitfire PR Mk XIs are currently airworthy in the UK. PL965 is based at former RAF Battle of Britain aerodrome, North Weald, and operated by Peter Teichman. Spitfire PR XI PL983 is based at Duxford and operated by the Aircraft Restoration Company. The PR MK XI was the fastest Merlin-engine Spitfire ever built.

From February 1944, photo-reconnaissance activity intensified further. Several reconnaissance flights had been tasked with photographing the Normandy area, to mark out enemy defences and possible paratrooper landing zones. Flying alone and unarmed deep into enemy territory was not for the faint-hearted. Fortunately, the adapted Spitfires were amongst the fastest aeroplanes of the time and could fly at altitudes beyond the reach of enemy fighters.

Supermarine Spitfire PR XI PL983 (G-PRXI) known as 'L' wears the wartime photo-reconnaissance blue livery of its time, serving in Europe

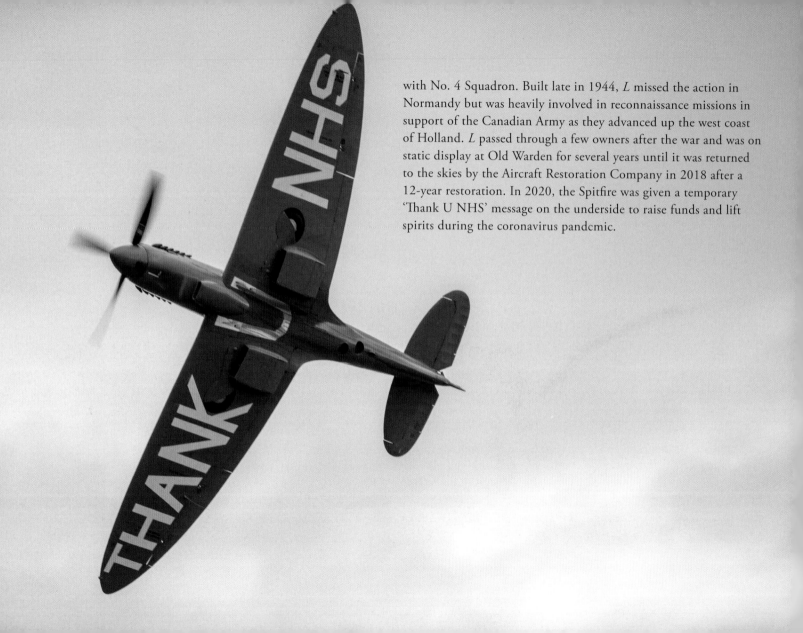

with No. 4 Squadron. Built late in 1944, *L* missed the action in Normandy but was heavily involved in reconnaissance missions in support of the Canadian Army as they advanced up the west coast of Holland. *L* passed through a few owners after the war and was on static display at Old Warden for several years until it was returned to the skies by the Aircraft Restoration Company in 2018 after a 12-year restoration. In 2020, the Spitfire was given a temporary 'Thank U NHS' message on the underside to raise funds and lift spirits during the coronavirus pandemic.

The development of the photo-reconnaissance Spitfire started in 1939 when several Spitfires had their guns removed and were fitted with additional fuel tanks and cameras in an operation led by Sidney Cotton at Heston Aerodrome. By the spring of 1940, the modified Spitfires could reach Berlin and back in one four-and-a-half-hour trip. The designs evolved further, and the PR Mk XI was able to operate at altitudes over 30,000ft and could fly at speeds of around 400mph. As such, the PR Mk XI was the fastest of all the Merlin-powered Spitfires.

Supermarine Spitfire PR Mk XI PL965 was built at Aldermaston factory in the summer of 1944. Later that year PL965 was allocated to No. 16 Squadron, which at the time was based near

Brussels in Belgium. PL965 was given the identifying code 'R' for Robert and the markings it still wears today. Towards the end of the war, PL965 was tasked with photographing enemy territory for bomb damage and to monitor airfields harbouring jet and rocket-propelled aircraft.

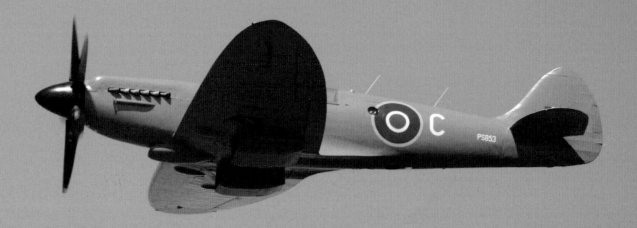

The PR Mk XI was the most numerous of the D-Day reconnaissance Spitfires, but in the quest for more range, more height and more speed the development did not stop there. Shortly before the Normandy landings, the PR Mk XIX Spitfires began to enter service. These were powered by Griffon engines and could fly at over 42,000ft at a speed of 445mph.

Often referred to as the 'Rolls-Royce' Spitfire because it belongs to the car and aero-engine giants, PS853 is a PR Mk XIX Spitfire that is well-known on the airshow circuit. Operated by the BBMF for several decades before Rolls-Royce acquired the iconic aeroplane in 1996. It was originally delivered to the RAF in January 1945, a little too late for D-Day, but it represents the pinnacle of photo-reconnaissance Spitfire development. A handful of these marks would have entered service in time for action over Normandy.

A replica V1 rocket and launch pad at IWM Duxford.

One of the most important jobs given to the photo-reconnaissance units was the identification of the V1 and V2 rocket sites. The Allied commanders were particularly concerned about this unknown threat and were fearful that the rockets could be brought to bear on the invasion fleet. It was therefore deemed essential that these were identified so that the bombers could neutralise the threats. During Operation *Crossbow,* the PR flights identified numerous V1 and V2 sites which were subsequently targeted by bombers. Hindsight shows that the rockets were no direct threat to the invasion fleet, but they did inflict significant damage to southern England throughout the final years of the war.

The BBMF also operates two PR Mk XIX Spitfires. Although both were too late to see service in the Second World War, they are occasionally given period markings to commemorate those who served during the conflict. PM631 is pictured here paying tribute to the very early PR Mk XIX Spitfires operating over Europe in June 1944. The markings of No. 541 Squadron complete with D-Day invasion stripes pay homage to the brave reconnaissance pilots of the D-Day period.

The prototype de Havilland DH98 Mosquito on display at the de Havilland Aircraft Museum.

photo-reconnaissance aircraft. Despite doubts from the Air Ministry, the Mosquito proved so capable it was soon adopted for several different roles within the RAF.

The de Havilland Mosquito was considered one of the most successful aircraft of the whole war. Built almost entirely of wood, it was lightweight, easy to construct and very fast. The Mosquito undertook several roles during the Normandy landings, but its speed made it ideal for photo-reconnaissance. It was light, agile and capable of carrying a heavy load, making it an ideal platform for large fuel tanks and heavy cameras – perfect for long photographic sorties deep in enemy territory.

From March 1944, the area directly over Normandy was being photographed once every three days, to note the ever-changing developments in Rommel's so-called Atlantic line. The de Havilland DH98 Mosquito was initially designed as a light bomber but at the Air Ministry's request, some of the first production models were built as

Due to its wooden structure, very few Mosquitos have stood the test of time. Almost 8,000 were built but only around 30 remain today. There are just three surviving photo-reconnaissance variants in the world: two in Australia and one in South Africa. In the UK, a range of Mosquitos are on show, and there are currently two projects to restore a Mosquito to flight.

The USAAF were also involved in photo-reconnaissance missions. They too operated Spitfires, but the twin-engine P38 Lightning was also converted into the F-5E variant for low-level photographic sorties. In perilous so-called 'dicing' missions, the F-5Es would be flown low over the proposed landing beaches to capture 180-degree angle images of the enemy defences. More than 500 examples of the F-5E were produced. Capable of over 410mph and very stable due to its counter-rotating engines, the F-5E was ideal for daring low-level photography missions.

This P-38 Lightning (N25Y) was manufactured in 1944. It was originally built as a F-5G photo-reconnaissance variant, but it has been reconfigured several times in its lifetime. N25Y has maintained the same registration since being struck off from the United States Air Force in September 1945. It has had a colourful post-war career including second place in the 1947 Miami Air Race before falling into the ownership of decorated Second World War pilot Marvin 'Lefty' Gardner. It is currently owned and operated by the Flying Bulls from Salzburg Airport in Austria.

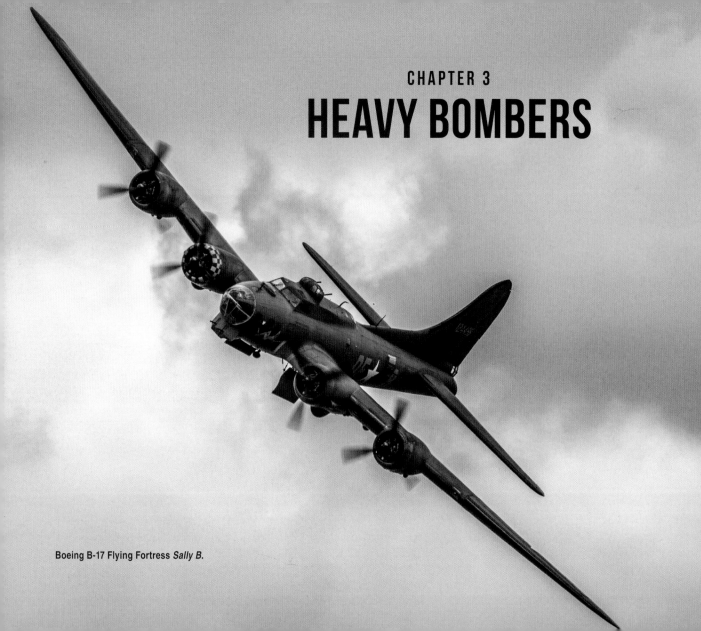

CHAPTER 3
HEAVY BOMBERS

Boeing B-17 Flying Fortress *Sally B.*

From as early as 1943, the combined Allied forces began a heavy bombing campaign with one eye on an invasion. Directive *Pointblank* was issued on 3 June 1943 in response to an increase in enemy fighter aircraft activity across Europe. The directive was primarily to focus on the destruction of the Luftwaffe, including its aircraft, airfields, repair depots and factories. The two-pronged approach saw daylight raids by the US Eighth Air Force and night-time bombing by RAF Bomber Command. *Pointblank* was generally considered successful.

By the beginning of 1944, enemy aircraft numbers in the skies had dwindled; the beginning phases of the invasion could commence.

The US forces primary bomber was the enigmatic Boeing B-17 Flying Fortress (pictured above left), but several squadrons of Consolidated B-24 Liberators and Martin B-26 Marauders were also put to good use throughout the campaign. The RAF also had three heavy bombers in service at the time: the Short Stirling, Handley Page Halifax and the Avro Lancaster (pictured above right).

The Boeing B-17 Flying Fortress has gained legendary status for its heroics during the Second World War. It served with the USAAF and the RAF and was the backbone of the AEAF in the build up to D-Day. Known for its heavy armament and ability to absorb a huge amount of punishment and still fly home, it truly deserved the Flying Fortress name. The B-17 was responsible for almost half of the 1.5 million tons of bombs dropped on Nazi Germany by US aircraft.

There is only one B-17 still airworthy in Europe. It has been operated by Elly Sallingboe since 1982 and is known affectionately as *Sally B* in her honour. *Sally B* was built in 1945, too late for wartime service but was used for training and research duties in the US before moving to the Institut Géographique National in France for survey and mapping work. *Sally B* has been based in the UK since 1975 and currently resides at Duxford. For the finale of the display, *Sally B* usually trails smoke

from two engines as a tribute to the wartime crews who suffered heavy losses over Germany.

The B-17 was equipped with four Wright R-18200-97 Cyclone radial engines and 13 machine guns, and it was capable of 287mph at 25,000ft. On the build-up to D-Day, the US B-17s were tasked with high-risk daylight raids and were often accompanied by fighters such as the P47

Thunderbolt (as pictured above) for protection. From January 1944 onwards, the provisional date of 1 May had been set for the invasion. Once this was finalised, the Allied heavy bombing forces were organised through a strategic bombing committee. Lieutenant General Carl Spaatz took command of both the US Eighth (based in England) and Fifteenth (based in Italy) Air Forces so that all efforts could be concentrated on *Overlord*.

Throughout March 1944, the American heavy bombers attacked a range of targets developing their own pathfinder techniques to allow greater accuracy. Significantly, the first daylight raid on Berlin also took place during this month. Seven hundred and thirty bombers took part in the raid, but because of limited fuel range at that time, fighter aircraft were not able to provide cover for the whole flight. Lack of fighter support during the day in central Germany left the B-17s vulnerable to the Luftwaffe and, as such, losses were high.

The Imperial War Museum's (IWM) B-17 was built at Douglas Long Beach as B-17G. Originally it was given the US military serial 44-83735. It saw no active service, but, like *Sally B*, it was one of the B-17s chosen to go to France for survey and mapping work. It now wears the livery of 44-238133 *Reluctant Dragon* which operated several missions over Europe in 1944. It suffered severe damage one month before D-Day in a raid over Berlin but was able to limp home. After repairs, 44-238133 was back in action until being reported missing in action on 30 November 1944 after another raid over Berlin.

The Consolidated B-24 Liberator was the second of three heavy American bombers in service during the Normandy campaign. It was a versatile aircraft with an impressive range, making it suitable for many different types of operation. Around 18,500 Liberators were built in total. During the period leading up to D-Day, Liberators were used extensively for daylight bombing raids, often using the new radio-guided munition system known as Azon.

Liberators were also chosen for 'carpetbagging' missions where spies and commandos would be dropped into France to undertake covert missions. Dangerous low-level night-time sorties would also try to recover crews who had been shot down. It is thought that over 5,000 men were rescued in this way. The skills developed by the pilots during this period were also put to good use following the successful invasion when Liberators were tasked with supplying gasoline to the frontline forces. During the summer of 1944, over 800,000 US gallons were delivered to General George Patton's Army.

Two complete Liberators survive in the UK today. One can be found at the RAF Museum in Hendon and the other resides at IWM Duxford in Cambridgeshire. The IWM's Liberator (pictured here) was built too late to see active wartime service but was used as a research aircraft for almost ten years before becoming a gate guardian at Lackland Air Force Base. It arrived in the UK in 1999.

At the beginning of March 1944, RAF Bomber Command received instructions to carry out a series of attacks on French marshalling yards to interrupt the German transportation networks. Over 250 Handley Page Halifax bombers were chosen to lead the attack with support from the Mosquito pathfinders. Attacks on railways continued through March and were largely successful in the disruption of Germany's goods transportation network. However, high French civilian casualties were an unacceptable cause for alarm, so the strategy was rethought for April.

Very few Halifax's have survived, but there is a complete one in Canada and a reconstructed airframe at the Yorkshire Air Museum in England. This nose section of PN323, a Mk VII Halifax, is currently undergoing work at the IWM in Duxford. It was built by the Fairey aviation company and joined No. 29 Maintenance Unit (MU) in the RAF in September 1945. It was struck off charge in 1948, but the front section was saved from scrap by the Skyframe Collection in 1965.

The Handley Page Halifax took its first flight in 1939 and entered RAF service in November the following year. The bomber was initially powered by four Rolls-Royce Merlin engines, but later models were more commonly given Bristol Hercules powerplants. The heavy bomber performed well for the RAF throughout the war but was generally considered inferior to the Lancaster due to a more limited bomb bay. As such it was widely used for other duties including as a glider-towing tug for the Normandy invasion.

The RAF Museum's Halifax did not survive long enough to be part of the D-Day invasions, but W1048 is significant in its own right. It was one of the 31 Halifax bombers to raid the German battleship *Tirpitz*. Sadly during its 3am attack on 27 April 1942, W1048 was hit by intense flak causing an outer starboard engine fire. Brave pilot Don MacIntyre completed a wheels-up landing on a frozen Lake Hoklingen in Norway. The aircraft sank soon after but was recovered in 1973. It is now displayed as a preserved wreckage at Hendon.

The Avro Lancaster has achieved a near mythical status based on its exploits during the Second World War. The four-engine bomber took leading roles in many of the RAF's most iconic and daring missions, including legendary dam-busting raids. Initially it was designed as a two-engine bomber known as the Avro Manchester, but poor performance led to a rethink. The Lancaster boasted outstanding performance and reliability alongside a huge bomb bay, which made it the most successful of the RAF's heavy bombers.

Over 15 Lancasters have survived intact across the world. Four can be seen on display in the UK. The UK's only airworthy Lancaster is operated by the BBMF. Although it did not see operational service in the war, it is currently painted to represent two separate aircraft, both operational during June 1944.

The port side represents *Leader* from 460 Squadron (Royal Australian Air Force), an aircraft that completed 94 operations between May and August 1944. The starboard side represents the Lancaster flown by former BBMF OC Andy Millikin's grandfather between May and July 1944.

In April 1944, the bombing campaign was refocused on targets that were considered directly important to the planned invasion. The main priority was the railways, followed by the V-weapon sites (known as 'Noball' targets). Third priority was the industrial sites, closely followed by the occupied airfields. The bombing offensive was carried out by numerous aircraft types, but it was the Lancaster, carrying the heaviest payload of all the heavy bombers, that was responsible for a considerable part of the destruction.

For a heavy bomber of that period, the Lancaster was considered relatively agile. It was also capable of 282mph with a range of 2,500 miles. It could comfortably operate at 21,000ft but was also called upon for very low-level missions too. The Lancaster pictured here is based at the IWM in Duxford. It entered service at the beginning of 1945 and had a quiet war but was eventually converted for maritime reconnaissance in Canada where it was originally built.

As D-Day approached, the heavy bombers were tasked with targeting the coastal defence batteries and radar sites to clear the way for the invasion. In the final stages, heavy bombers were sent to active airfields to ensure that the Luftwaffe would not hamper the invasion in any way. By D-Day minus one, the combined forces had dropped almost 200,000 tons of bombs. RAF Bomber Command claimed almost half of this payload, thanks in part to the impressive bomb bays of the Lancaster.

An exciting ongoing project to return Avro Lancaster NX611 *Just Jane* to the skies is gathering pace at the East Kirkby Aviation Museum in Lincolnshire. The museum was initially set up by two farming brothers, Fred and Harold Panton, who lost their eldest brother during his service for Bomber Command in the Second World War. Although NX611 did not serve during the war, it is worthy of a mention, as it is the only Lancaster in the UK in which the public can undertake a taxi ride, and with public support it could soon become airworthy.

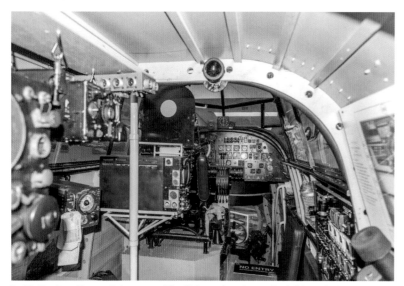

Inside the Avro Museum's Lancaster. The flight engineer's seat is visible at the bottom right of the image.

Avro Lancaster pilot's view, Avro Heritage Museum.

The Avro Lancaster housed seven crew members during a typical operation. The pilot sat in an armoured chair just behind the nose of the aircraft. There was no co-pilot (since 1942, the flight-engineer had replaced this role to conserve costs). The excessive losses of crew on dangerous bombing missions had made it impossible to supply two trained pilots for every Lancaster. The flight engineer occupied a fold-out seat to the right of the pilot. He would monitor instruments and assist with throttle controls.

The rest of the crew was made up of two gunners, a bomb-aimer, navigator and wireless operator. The bomb-aimer was responsible for manning the front guns until he would adopt the prone position to peer through the sight on immediate approach to the target. There would also be a mid-gunner on the lookout for enemy aircraft, with his unique view in the upper turret. The navigator occupied a tight space where he would pour over maps and compasses with limited assistance from temperamental electronic aids. The wireless operator would monitor incoming communications and relay messages to base if required. Finally, the rear gunner sat at the very tail end of the aircraft in a cold space too tight to even wear a parachute.

The Avro museum houses this replica Lancaster front section, which is built of original artefacts. The original aircraft, R5868 *S-Sugar*,

Above left: Avro Lancaster wireless operator's station, Avro Heritage Museum.

Above right: Avro Lancaster bomb aimer's position, Avro Heritage Museum.

Right: The RAF Museum's Avro Lancaster R5868 *S-Sugar*.

can be seen at the RAF Museum in Hendon. R5868 was one of only 35 Lancasters to complete 100 missions in the Second World War. It took part in the bombing of German coastal defences on D-Day and was also one of the first aircraft to bring home prisoners of war following the German surrender.

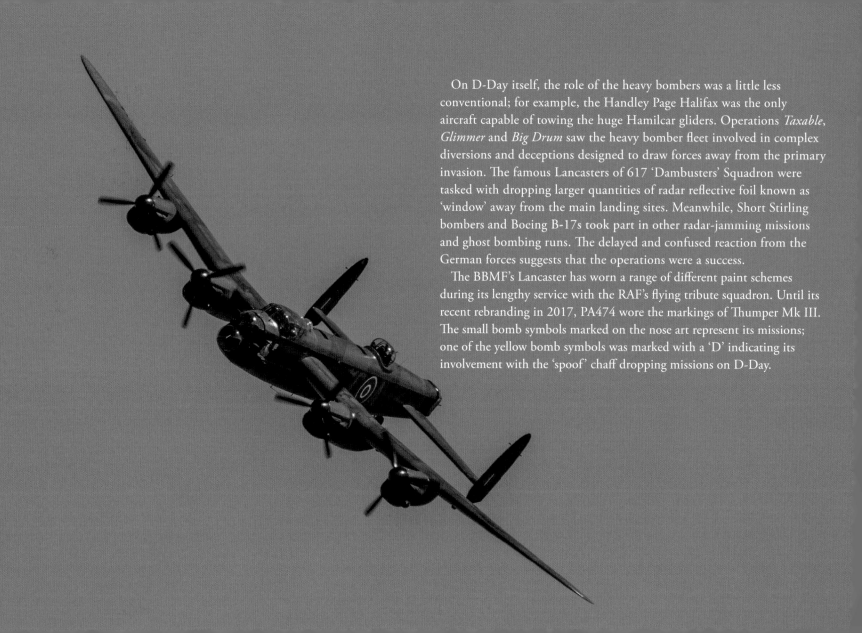

On D-Day itself, the role of the heavy bombers was a little less conventional; for example, the Handley Page Halifax was the only aircraft capable of towing the huge Hamilcar gliders. Operations *Taxable*, *Glimmer* and *Big Drum* saw the heavy bomber fleet involved in complex diversions and deceptions designed to draw forces away from the primary invasion. The famous Lancasters of 617 'Dambusters' Squadron were tasked with dropping larger quantities of radar reflective foil known as 'window' away from the main landing sites. Meanwhile, Short Stirling bombers and Boeing B-17s took part in other radar-jamming missions and ghost bombing runs. The delayed and confused reaction from the German forces suggests that the operations were a success.

The BBMF's Lancaster has worn a range of different paint schemes during its lengthy service with the RAF's flying tribute squadron. Until its recent rebranding in 2017, PA474 wore the markings of Thumper Mk III. The small bomb symbols marked on the nose art represent its missions; one of the yellow bomb symbols was marked with a 'D' indicating its involvement with the 'spoof' chaff dropping missions on D-Day.

Together, the combined AEAFs were able to deliver much destruction to the German defences. Railways, transport networks, airfields, coastal defences and radar stations were all significantly effected in preparation for the invasion. Although it was not always that simple, the Americans tended to operate during daylight, whilst the RAF continued the campaign throughout the night.

The British and American bomber aircraft fell into their niches nicely and were further modified throughout production to suit their intended roles. These two images show the direct comparison between the American Boeing B-17 and the British Avro Lancaster. The bomb bay on the Lancaster was far superior in size and suited the night-time heavy bomber raids. The B-17 was better designed for daylight raids. Better visibility allowed greater accuracy but required better defence of the aircraft which was achieved via its 13 machine-guns posts; the trade off being it could not carry as much weight in bombs.

CHAPTER 4

GROUND-ATTACK AIRCRAFT AND LIGHT BOMBERS

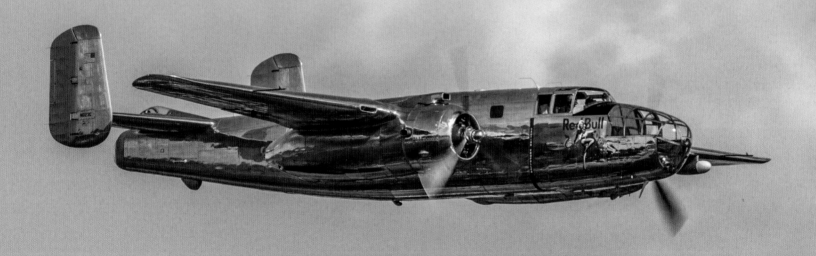

The Flying Bull's B-25 Mitchell.

In support of the heavy bombing campaign, the AEAF operated a range of light and medium bombers alongside its four-engine heavy bombers. Aircraft such as the Douglas Boston (known in America as the A-20 Havoc) and the B-26 Marauder played a significant role in the invasion, but sadly there are no complete survivors currently on display in the UK. The B-25 Mitchell is the sole representative of the American twin-engine bombers viewable in the UK. The Mitchell is synonymous with the famous Doolittle raids in the Pacific campaign, but it was not used by the USAAF in Europe.

However, over 900 Mitchells were in service with the RAF and were amongst the first aircraft moved to forward bases in northern France after the invasion.

There are several surviving B-25 Mitchells in the world today, including two on display in the UK: one at the IWM in Duxford (pictured above left), the other at the RAF Museum in Hendon (pictured above right). There are also a couple of airworthy Mitchells in Europe, including one based in Austria with the Flying Bulls. All of the surviving aircraft featured here are B-25J variants that were too late to see active service in the war.

The prototype de Havilland Mosquito on display at the de Havilland Aircraft Museum.

A bomber variant de Havilland Mosquito, TA634, later converted to a target tug aircraft. Just visible in the background is the fighter-bomber FB Mk VI Mosquito at the de Havilland Aircraft Museum.

During the early stages, there were often clear distinctions between fighting, training and bombing aircraft, but as the war evolved the air forces on both sides had to adapt quickly to keep pace with the enemy. This meant that some aircraft would be required to deviate from their intended purpose, whilst others became versatile multi-role aircraft capable of bombing, fighting and photo-reconnaissance. The de Havilland Mosquito is a prime example: although a superb fighter it was also used for ground attack, paving the way for the land armies on D-Day and beyond.

There are around 30 surviving Mosquitos in the world today, including two airworthy examples in America although ongoing projects will see this number increase soon. A handful can be seen on static display in the UK. The RAF Museum has Mosquitos viewable on both of its sites, and there is a superb example of a target tug variant at Duxford. Pictured here are the three aircraft that are on display at the de Havilland Museum at London Colney. The first is particularly significant as the original prototype Mosquito built in 1940.

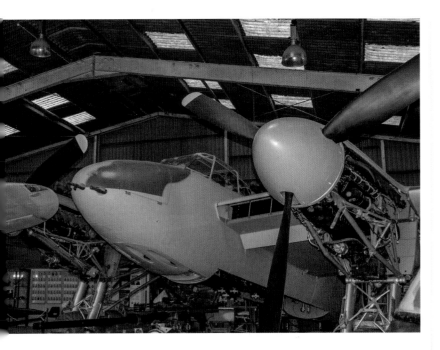

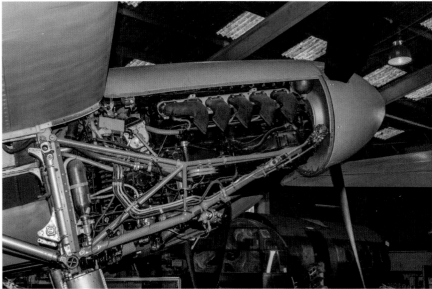

One of the Merlin engines of de Havilland FB VI Mosquitos, TA122, an Airspeed Horsa glider fuselage is just visible in the background.

The most widely-used variant of the de Havilland Mosquito during the Normandy campaign was the FB Mk VI fighter-bomber. It was intended for 'intruder' strike missions. With four .303 Browning machine guns in its nose and four 20mm cannon in its belly, it was a potent weapon. Its supercharged Rolls-Royce Merlin engines and light wooden structure without onboard radar and pressurised cabin made it lightweight and very fast. During preparations for D-Day the Second Tactical Air Force operated numerous FB VI Mosquitos and targeted power stations, communications centres and V-weapon sites.

The de Havilland Museum looks after one of the few remaining FB VI Mosquitos, TA122. It was built at the de Havilland factory and design facility in Hatfield. It was taken on charge with the RAF on 10 March 1945. It was too late for the D-Day invasions, but it did operate out of Belgium and Holland in the final stages of the Second World War. TA122 was finally struck off charge on 30 June 1950. Although taken apart for spares, its fuselage survived and was eventually paired up with the wings from a TR33 Mosquito, TW233, before going on display.

The de Havilland Mosquito was often referred to as the 'Wooden Wonder', but its primary construction material, wood, was considered by many to be an obsolete material for aircraft construction at the time. However, the lightweight twin-engine aircraft proved reliable, fast and agile; it was therefore capable of numerous roles. Mosquitos supported heavy bombers as both fighter escorts and pathfinders. Mosquitos could be fitted with a range of electronic aids and airborne radar which would help to locate enemy aircraft or pinpoint bombing targets. Once the targets were located, incendiary bombs were dropped onto them, causing huge fires to light the way for the main force. It was also a phenomenal light bomber and ground-attack aircraft in its own right.

Mosquito NF11 HJ711 is owned by Tony Agar and is based at the East Kirkby Aviation Museum in Lincolnshire. It is the only Mosquito in the UK that can currently taxi under its own power. Although it is a mix of several aircraft, it takes the identity of its cockpit, which is thought to be HJ711. As a night-fighting aircraft that was operational during 1944, it is one of the most significant Mosquitos to survive today. HJ711 served with both Nos. 141 and 169 Squadrons but it was with No. 169 Squadron that HJ711 made the squadron's first kill on 30 January 1944 when Squadron Leader J A H Cooper shot down a Messerschmitt Bf 110 whilst patrolling west of Berlin.

The ultimate British ground-attack aircraft of the period was the Hawker Typhoon. Although initially conceived as an all-out fighter to replace the Hurricane, it was soon realised that its strengths lay elsewhere. Powered by a Napier Sabre engine and capable of well over 400mph, the Typhoon was considered by many to be the most able Allied ground-attack aircraft of the war. The Mk Ia was equipped with an incredible 12 forward-firing machine guns. The Mk Ib was even more formidable with four 20mm canon and an external bomb load of 2,000lb. During the weeks surrounding D-Day, the Typhoon was an indispensable asset to the Allies. It was capable of high-speed light-bombing runs, devastating ground attacks and could hold its own against enemy fighters. It was the Allies' favoured aircraft for the attacks on German radar stations.

Over 3,000 Typhoons were built, but only one is on display today. The RAF Museum's example is Hawker Typhoon Mk 1b MN235. It was built in 1944 but did not see action during the war. Instead it was sent to America for trials. It's career in the US was short: after only nine hours of flight time it was placed in storage. MN235 now wears the markings of 440 Squadron (RCAF) which includes underwing D-Day stripes. Although this is currently the only complete survivor, an ongoing high-profile restoration project could see a Second World War combat veteran (Typhoon RB396) returned to the skies in the UK very soon.

In a campaign opened on 24 May 1944, 36 major bridges linking northern France to Paris and beyond were destroyed by the AEAF to prevent German reinforcements positioning for a counter-attack. Although larger bombers dropped over 5,000 tons of bombs onto the targeted bridges, it was the nimble, rugged fighter-bombers of the Eighth Air Force that proved to be the experts in this field. More specifically, the Republic P-47 Thunderbolt was ideally suited to the task. Between D-Day and VE day, the Thunderbolt pilots claimed to have destroyed 86,000 railroad cars, 9,000 locomotives, 6,000 armoured vehicles and 68,000 trucks.

Republic P-47 Thunderbolt G-THUN is a well-known aircraft on the UK airshow circuit. It was a former member of the Fighter Collection's fleet until it relocated to the USA in 2007. In 2018, it returned to the UK to join Richard Grace's impressive warbird line-up at Air Leasing, based at Sywell Aerodrome. G-THUN was built in 1945 at Republic's factory in Indiana. Initially it was given the serial number 45-49192. Service with the USAAF was brief although it did serve with the Air Training Command during the last few months of the war.

When kitted out in its fighter-bomber ground-attack configuration, the P-47 Thunderbolt could carry a bomb load of 2,500 pounds and an impressive array of five-inch rockets. Fully loaded, the P-47 weighed eight tons, making it one of the heaviest fighters of the war. The powerful Pratt & Whitney R-2800 Double Wasp engine ensured that the Thunderbolt was able to quickly evade the often intense enemy defences that were frequently encountered on the low-level bridge-busting missions.

G-THUN is currently painted as F4-J, *Nellie B,* from the 492 Fighter Squadron, which saw service over Europe from early on in 1944. The squadron played a pivotal role in the bombing and ground-attack missions that paved the way for the Normandy invasions. When the aircraft arrived in the UK it was simply know as *Nellie,* but after further research and photographic evidence the '*B*' was added for historical accuracy. Today the 492 Fighter Squadron is still based in the UK at RAF Lakenheath, and as a tribute to its past, three modern F-15 jets were given D-Day markings for the 75th anniversary year.

air victories – an impressive tally even for a pure-breed fighter. German Luftwaffe ace Heinz Bär also noted the P-47s astonishing ability to absorb punishment and was always wary of taking one on in combat.

Although there are several Republic P-47 Thunderbolts still intact across the world, only three are currently viewable in the UK. Aside from the airworthy Thunderbolt *Nellie B*, there are static examples at the RAF Museum in Hendon and at the IWM in Duxford. 45-49295 at the RAF Museum is painted in South East Asia campaign markings but 45-49192 (pictured here) in the American Air Museum at Duxford represents a D-Day Thunderbolt. It is presented as P-47D 42-26413 *Oregon's Britannia* which was the first P-47 with the 180-degree vision canopy. *Oregon's Britannia* was the personal aircraft of Colonel Hubert Zemke who served with the 56th Fighter Group across the Normandy campaign.

Although it was primarily employed as a ground-attack aircraft, the P-47 was far from a one-trick pony. For many American pilots, it was their first choice as an out-and-out fighter aircraft. Throughout the war, P-47 Thunderbolts, also known as 'Jugs', claimed almost 4,000 air-to-

The Lockheed P-38 Lightning earned the nickname the 'Fork-tailed Devil' from the German Luftwaffe pilots facing it in combat. It was used in multiple combat roles during the war but proved itself as a highly capable fighter-bomber. During the Normandy invasion, several Lightnings were assigned to the IX Tactical Air Command of the 370th and 474th Fighter Groups shortly before D-Day. They flew dive-bombing missions, targeting radar installations, enemy armour, troop concentrations and flak towers. Allegedly, Howard Nichols, the group commander, skipped a 500lb bomb through the front door of Field Marshal Günther von Kluge's headquarters whilst flying a Lightning in July 1944.

Less than 30 P-38 Lightnings have stood the test of time. Unsurprisingly, most of these are found in the United States. At present, the only P-38 that can be seen in Europe is the one owned and operated by the Flying Bulls in Salzburg, Austria. The unconventional twin tail makes it one of the most distinctive aircraft of the period. The two Allison engines with 1,600hp made the Lightning perfect for long-distance missions. Although there were a considerable number of Lightnings operating over Europe, it is better known for its role in the Pacific during the Second World War.

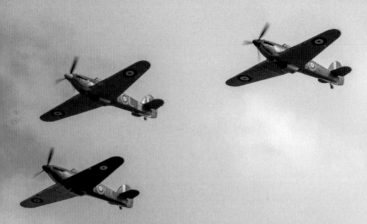

As tensions grew across Europe before the beginning of the war, pressure grew on the Air Ministry to supply new modern monoplane fighters. As such, the newly designed Hawker Hurricane was rushed into production. The decision to act quickly would ensure an ample supply of the early marks ready for combat, but it would ultimately cap the future design potential of the RAF's first 300mph fighter. Unlike the Spitfire, the Hurricane would be limited to just a handful of variants.

There are over 70 Hurricanes surviving across the world today in various states of preservation, from crash remains to fully restored flyers. In the UK, there are ten that are currently airworthy although thanks to the hard work of aircraft restorers, such as Hawker Restorations, the number is increasing. After the war, many Hurricanes were disposed of and soon there were hardly any left flying. In 2019, the Shuttleworth Military Airshow saw a modern-day record of seven Hawker Hurricanes in formation together. A sight not seen for 70 years.

The Hurricane had proved itself during the Battle of Britain; it made up the largest part of the aerial force that defended the country. As the war progressed, the Hurricane would be developed to take on several roles within the RAF. The ultimate development being the heavily-armed, menacing fighter-bomber. During the 1944 Normandy campaign, the Hurricane had largely been replaced by more advanced aircraft, but some Hurri-bombers were still sent out on ground-attack patrols during the period.

AG287 was built in Canada in 1942 and served with the Royal Canadian Air Force (RCAF) for 12 months before being converted to a Mk XII, which was essentially a Mk IIb Hurri-bomber with a Packard-built Merlin engine. It is currently painted in the markings of BE505. It can be seen here, ready to go with model bombs representing what it would have looked like during the war. BE505 has recently been converted into the world's only two-seat Hawker Hurricane, and passengers can now take flights out of Biggin Hill Aerodrome.

CHAPTER 5
FIGHTER AIRCRAFT

Two Supermarine Spitfires, ML407 and MH434, both wearing D-Day stripes.

Miss Helen, *Contrary Mary*, *Tall in the Saddle* and *The Shark* are currently the only four UK Airworthy Mustangs. *The Shark* has recently been repainted in a different colour scheme.

Control of the skies was a key requisite of a successful invasion; the Luftwaffe had failed to achieve this over Britain in 1940 and as such a German invasion was cancelled. The Allied commanders understood that army landing operations would be hampered unless the AEAF could master the European skies. To this end, a range of out-and-out fighter aircraft would be deployed on a series of sorties to provoke the Luftwaffe into action in the hope that they could be shot down. Fighter aircraft would also be vital in supporting heavy bombers across the Channel, as they too helped to eliminate key Luftwaffe targets on the ground. The AEAF would utilise all the air power at its disposal to ensure clear skies above the invasion grounds.

The North American P-51 Mustang was considered the most capable fighter aircraft in the American ranks in 1944. It was initially designed for the RAF in response to the War Cabinet's appeal for an American-built fighter aircraft during the early phases of the war. After its performance became apparent, the United States forces also adopted the Mustang, making it one of the most widely-used aircraft of the war. Numerous examples have survived, and many remain airworthy across the world. There are four currently airworthy in the UK (all pictured here) and a further four on static display in British museums. Ongoing restorations could see the UK airworthy total doubled very soon. Also, a handful of overseas visitors frequently boost the number of flying Mustangs visible in the UK for the summer airshow season.

North American Mustang P-51D G-SHWN makes a dramatic departure after refuelling at Tatenhill Airfield in Staffordshire.

In the autumn of 1943, the Allies realised that bombing alone was not going to eliminate the threat from the Luftwaffe. It would also require a concentrated effort from the fighter aircraft squadrons. Crossing the English Channel before fighting an aerial battle had proved a significant challenge for the Luftwaffe in 1940, as, because of the fuel range of the fighter aircraft, only limited combat time was permitted. The Allies were not going to make the same mistake. The North American P-51 Mustang showed promise as a fighter aircraft but did not realise its true potential until it was fitted with a Rolls-Royce Merlin. Suddenly, fuel economy had significantly increased. With the addition of extra fuel space, including optional drop tanks, the Allies had a fighter capable of 1,500 miles.

A close-up inspection of North American Mustang P-51D G-SHWN.

North American Mustang P-51D G-SHWN is owned by Shaun Patrick, operated by the Norwegian Spitfire Foundation and maintained by the Aircraft Restoration Company. For several years it has appeared as 'The Shark' wearing RAF markings, but recently this has been repainted to represent the Mustang flown by Colonel Donald Blakeslee, Commander of the Fourth Fighter Group. Blakeslee flew more combat missions than any other American fighter pilot and was credited with 14 and a half confirmed kills during the Second World War. During March of 1944, he led the Fourth Fighter group on several co-ordinated attacks on German industries. The Fourth became one of the first Allied fighter groups to fly over Berlin. On D-Day itself, the unit was very active, flying several fighter sweeps and dive-bombing missions, often becoming entangled with enemy fighters.

After intensive campaigns in the early part of 1944, the AEAF began to dominate the skies over northern Europe. The Luftwaffe was overrun with an influx of American fighter aircraft, combined with increased output from the British and Canadian aircraft industries. It is often thought that the Luftwaffe was a completely spent force by June 1944. However, evidence suggests that this was not entirely the case. The Allies certainly dominated the skies, but many aerial battles did take place on 6 June 1944 and Allied aircraft were shot down by enemy fighters as well as anti-aircraft flak from the ground.

North American Mustang P-51D N351MX was accepted into the Army Air Forces in 1945 and served in the US military until 1958. It is now operated by Comanche Fighters based in America but has recently visited Europe to perform at several airshows. Since 2018, N351MX has appeared as The Hun Hunter\Texas, which was flown by Captain Henry 'Baby' Brown of the

354th Fighter Squadron. Henry Brown was a highly decorated pilot who was very active during the Normandy campaign. He achieved ace status during the raids against the German oil industry in April 1944 and went on to serve until being shot down and captured in October that year.

During February 1944, the Allies launched what became known as the 'Big Week'. Repeated bombing of aircraft factories and airfields was combined with Allied fighter sweeps. This was an all-out effort to clear the skies for an invasion. Analysis has shown that the German aircraft industry was relatively unhampered by the bombing raids and continued with production. The impact of the fighter aircraft forces was considerably more measurable; over 2,500 German aircraft were lost throughout February, and although the German industry did continue to replace the aircraft lost, the loss of experienced fighter pilots was a severe blow to the Luftwaffe.

North American Mustang P-51D *Miss Helen* is one of the four airworthy Mustangs currently based in the UK. Dressed in authentic wartime markings, *Miss Helen* was delivered to the US Army Air Forces in 1945 and saw active service at the end of the Second World War with 352nd Fighter Group who became known as *The Blue Nosed Bastards of Bodney*. Although a little too late for D-Day, *Miss Helen* is known to have been flown by Captain Raymond Littge on several bombing escort missions into German territory, including one on 17 April 1945 where Captain Littge personally destroyed three Me109s and two Me262s on the ground.

At the time of the Normandy invasions, the P-51 Mustang was very much the preferred long-range fighter of the AEAF. Once the North American airframe had been paired up with a Merlin engine it was clear that this was a world-beating aircraft capable of escorting bombers to Berlin and back. On the evening of 5 June 1944, it was no surprise that the task of escorting the pre-invasion bombers was left largely to the Mustangs of the Eighth Fighter Command. The bombers were tasked with attacking the coastal defences ahead of the land-based forces, moving slowly ahead of the troops. The US Mustangs, along with a couple of squadrons of Thunderbolts met little opposition from the Luftwaffe so were able to assist the battering of land defences with strafing ground attacks.

One of the most significant airworthy Mustangs today is based around the remains of P-51B 43-24837, which crashed in Beckley after the pilot was forced to bale out during a training exercise just four days after D-Day. It is one of the few airworthy Mustangs today with the original Malcolm Hood canopy. It currently wears the markings of the Berlin Express, which was flown by the legendary American ace Bill Overstreet during the time of the Normandy invasions. Overstreet famously flew under the Eiffel Tower whilst successfully shooting down a Messerschmitt Me109 during 1944. Although based in the United States with Comanche Fighters, it has recently spent a significant amount of time displaying in Europe.

The Supermarine Spitfire was the dominant fighter within the RAF throughout 1944. Having already achieved legendary status during the Battle of Britain, the Spitfire was being continually upgraded into an ever-improving, sleek fighting machine. No other aircraft has achieved such mythical status. Twenty-four marks of Spitfire were produced in total and each mark had numerous variants. The final Griffon-engine Spitfires were twice as heavy, twice as powerful and could climb 80 per cent faster than the original Mk I built just ten years earlier. During the Normandy operations, Mk V and IX variants dominated the ranks, but there were also a few squadrons equipped with the Mk VII and the Mk XVI.

Around 250 Spitfires have survived in the world to this day. Around 60 are airworthy, with over half of these residing in the UK. There are also numerous examples in museums and several ongoing restoration projects, meaning that the airworthy numbers are likely to increase in time. This image shows 14 Spitfires (including one Seafire) performing at one of the IWM's airshows. Duxford Aerodrome has been synonymous with the Spitfire since it arrived there to equip the first RAF squadron in 1938. Today, it is now the home of the IWM, where sights of several Spitfires flying together are becoming increasingly common.

The Mk V Spitfire was initially considered an interim measure to counteract the rising threat from the Luftwaffe, whose developments with the Bf 109 were temporarily outclassing the RAF's best fighters. Whilst further, more dramatic developments were pondered at the Supermarine design centre, the Mk II airframe was hastily adapted to fit a Merlin 45 engine and fitted with wings capable of carrying drop fuel tanks or external bombs. The Mk V proved so effective that it became the most numerously produced Spitfire mark that was still widely in service on D-Day and beyond.

Supermarine Spitfire EE602 was built by Westland Aircraft in 1942. It is a Mk Vc variant, currently operated by the Biggin Hill Heritage Hangar. EE602 completed over 100 missions in the Second World War, including escorting the B-17 Flying Fortress *Memphis Belle* back to the English coast after her now famous 25th mission. As part of the 'Fund a Spitfire' scheme to help the war effort, many clubs and companies were able to buy their own Spitfire for £5,000. One such company, the Central Railway in Uruguay, ran by ex-pats, did so for EE602.

During the preparations for D-Day, the AEAF had largely been successful in clearing the skies for the invasion. Although there was some resistance from the Luftwaffe, some of the Allied fighters saw little action over the French skies on 6 June 1944. As such, the Supermarine Spitfire was called upon to support the Navy by flying low over the beaches to help direct the artillery fire. Many Spitfires were also called upon to support the ground troops with sweeping low-level attacks on fortification and enemy vehicles just ahead of the invasion.

Supermarine Spitfire Mk Vb AB910 has had an outstanding career, including over three years of frontline service with the RAF. Built at the Castle Bromwich factory near Birmingham in 1941, Spitfire AB910 was thrown into action straightaway but given a short respite after a minor landing accident at Lymphe. Following repair, AB910 was moved to convoy protection and eventually gained some invasion experience in the fierce aerial battles over Dieppe during the ill-fated 1942 raids. AB910 flew operationally until July 1944, taking part in an incredible 143 missions, including several cover patrols over the Normandy beaches on D-Day itself. It is now operated by the RAF's BBMF and is currently painted in the colour scheme of a 64 Squadron Spitfire with full invasion stripes as worn on 6 June 1944.

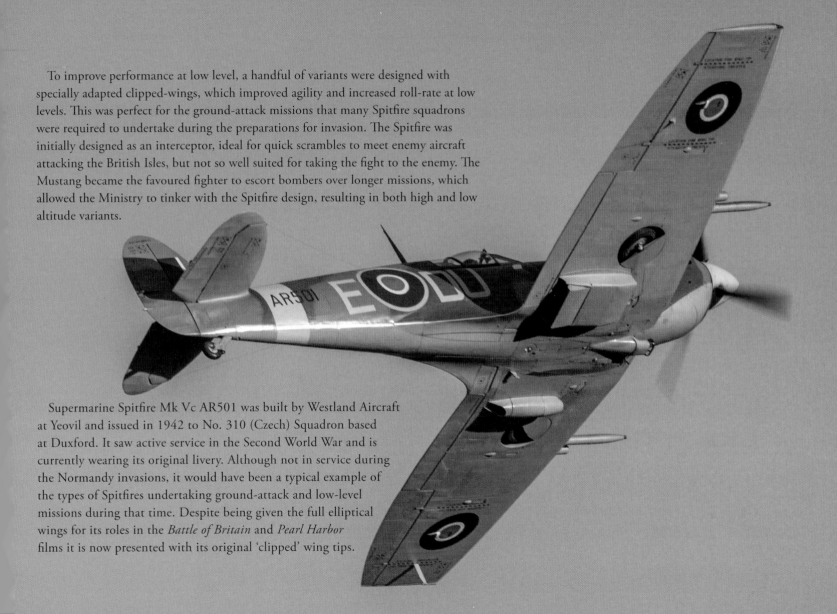

To improve performance at low level, a handful of variants were designed with specially adapted clipped-wings, which improved agility and increased roll-rate at low levels. This was perfect for the ground-attack missions that many Spitfire squadrons were required to undertake during the preparations for invasion. The Spitfire was initially designed as an interceptor, ideal for quick scrambles to meet enemy aircraft attacking the British Isles, but not so well suited for taking the fight to the enemy. The Mustang became the favoured fighter to escort bombers over longer missions, which allowed the Ministry to tinker with the Spitfire design, resulting in both high and low altitude variants.

Supermarine Spitfire Mk Vc AR501 was built by Westland Aircraft at Yeovil and issued in 1942 to No. 310 (Czech) Squadron based at Duxford. It saw active service in the Second World War and is currently wearing its original livery. Although not in service during the Normandy invasions, it would have been a typical example of the types of Spitfires undertaking ground-attack and low-level missions during that time. Despite being given the full elliptical wings for its roles in the *Battle of Britain* and *Pearl Harbor* films it is now presented with its original 'clipped' wing tips.

Supermarine Spitfire Mk Vb EP120 is another example of the low-flying clipped-winged variant. It achieved seven kills during the Second World War, making it one of the most credited Spitfires still flying today. EP120 was built at the Castle Bromwich factory where it was also test flown by Alex Henshaw. It was taken on charge by the RAF in May 1942 and was assigned to 501 Squadron the following month. Six of EP120's confirmed kills were with Squadron Leader Geoffrey Northcott at the helm.

In April 1944, Supermarine Spitfire EP120 was taken on charge with No. 402 'City of Winnipeg' (RCAF) Squadron. EP120 was operational for the D-Day preparations but returned to No. 33 MU at Lyneham just before D-Day itself. It still wears its original colours and code AE-A from this period today. After an impressive frontline career, EP120 was rewarded with semi-retirement as a ground instructional airframe for the final year of the Second World War. EP120 was returned to the skies in September 1995 and is now operated by the Fighter Collection, based at Duxford Aerodrome in Cambridgeshire.

At the beginning of 1942 the Focke-Wulf Fw 190 of the German Luftwaffe began to dominate the skies. Although the Mk V Spitfire

would continue in service in some form until the end of the war, it was clearly no match for the new German fighter. To combat this, Rolls-Royce devised a two-staged supercharged Merlin engine which would be fitted to the modified Spitfire airframe to produce the impressive Mk IX. Test pilot Jeffrey Quill described this as a quantum leap in performance. The Mk IX provided many advantages over the Mk V, especially at high altitude. The Mk IX became the most widely-used variant during the D-Day operations.

MH434 is a Mk IXb Spitfire that was built in 1943. It is one of the most famous Spitfires of all time, having a remarkable war record and equally impressive post-war career, including starring roles in many films and TV shows such as the 1969 *Battle of Britain* movie. MH434 entered RAF service in the summer of 1943. It was built at the Castle Bromwich factory and tested by the legendary Alex Henshaw. MH434 was credited with a kill on 27 August 1943 when Flight Lieutenant Henry Lardner-Burke shot down a Focke-Wulf Fw-190 and damaged a second during a mission escorting the B-17 Flying Fortresses of the USAAF.

In 1944, MH434 was assigned to pilot Flight Sergeant Alfred 'Bill' Burge. He flew 12 operational sorties in MH434 before the squadron's existing Mk IXs were all exchanged for new Spitfires that could carry rockets for use in ground-attack sorties. After over 80 operational sorties, MH434 was stood down in March 1945, after seeing extensive action throughout the time of the Allied invasion and beyond. It is now operated by the Old Flying Machine Company and is based at Duxford Aerodrome.

The BBMF operates several historic aircraft as part of the RAF's own tribute flight. Based at RAF Coningsby, the BBMF are fortunate to host two veterans of the Normandy invasions, including Supermarine Spitfire MK356. MK356 is a low-flying Mk IXe Spitfire that was built in Castle Bromwich early in 1944. Having been briefly kitted out at RAF Cosford, MK356 soon moved to the recently formed No. 433 (RCAF) Squadron. 433 Squadron were known as the Hornet Squadron and were part of the 144 Canadian Wing. Along with the rest of the squadron, MK356 became part of the Second Tactical Air Force that moved around substantially over the period of the Allied invasion.

During the preparations for invasion, MK356 took part in several fighter-bomber sweeps and bomber escort missions over northern France. In fact, MK356 took part in 60 missions in 60 days during this period. The damage sustained during this time is still visible on the aircraft today. On 6 June 1944, MK356 undertook three beach patrols over Normandy in support of the invasion. The following day (D-Day +1) Canadian Flying Officer Gordon Ockenden shared a kill of a Bf 109 in MK356 just off the Normandy coast. Just eight days later, after an unfortunate belly landing, MK356's war was over. The historic Spitfire would not fly again for over 50 years. Although presently painted in a desert camouflage scheme, MK356 was displayed for many years in the D-Day invasion stripes of 126 Squadron.

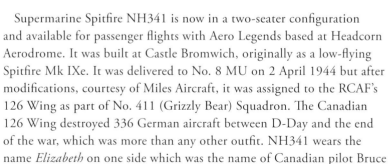

Supermarine Spitfire NH341 is now in a two-seater configuration and available for passenger flights with Aero Legends based at Headcorn Aerodrome. It was built at Castle Bromwich, originally as a low-flying Spitfire Mk IXe. It was delivered to No. 8 MU on 2 April 1944 but after modifications, courtesy of Miles Aircraft, it was assigned to the RCAF's 126 Wing as part of No. 411 (Grizzly Bear) Squadron. The Canadian 126 Wing destroyed 336 German aircraft between D-Day and the end of the war, which was more than any other outfit. NH341 wears the name *Elizabeth* on one side which was the name of Canadian pilot Bruce

Whiteford's wife. Whiteford flew NH341 for the first time less than one week after D-Day. He would go on to make more flights in NH431 than any other wartime pilot.

In NH341's first sortie on 12 June 1944, pilot Bruce Whiteford helped escort 220 Avro Lancaster bombers on a mission to attack Le Havre port. Whiteford noted the mission for the 'bags of flak and fire' which he encountered on the treacherous journey there and back. Fortunately, he made it back safely and MH341 would make a further 26 operational combat flights over the post-D-Day battlefields during the Normandy campaign.

ML407, the *Grace Spitfire* with temporary D-Day stripes over the No. 485 Squadron markings it wore in 1944.

Supermarine Spitfire ML407 has claim to be the most significant of the surviving D-Day fighters. It was built at the Birmingham Castle Bromwich shadow factory in early 1944. It flew a total of 176 operational combat sorties, totalling almost 400 combat hours during the Second World War. Most significantly, Flying Officer Johnnie Houlton was credited with the first enemy aircraft shot down over the Normandy beaches; he was flying ML407. In 1950, the iconic Spitfire was converted into a two-seat configuration for the Irish Air Corps as an advanced trainer.

ML407 was delivered to No. 485 (New Zealand) Squadron on 29 April 1944 by the famous female Air Transport Auxiliary pilot Jackie Moggridge. This Spitfire embraced the multinational theme in the Allied forces by serving with various squadrons including No. 308 (Polish) Squadron, No. 349 (Belgian) Squadron, No. 341 (Free French) Squadron and No. 332 (Norwegian) Squadron, before being transferred back to No. 485 (New Zealand) Squadron at the end of the war. The aircraft has been in the capable hands of the Grace family since 1979. Enthusiasts can now take a passenger flight in this historic aircraft. It has come to be known as the 'Grace Spitfire' and has appeared in several different identities.

The Hawker Tempest was one of the most powerful British fighters to see service in the Second World War. It extended the boundaries of piston-engine aircraft and provided another quantum leap in performance. It was designed to be fast and manoeuvrable and was very heavily armed. Although a very new aircraft in 1944, some were ready in time to equip Nos. 3 and 486 Squadrons of the Second Tactical Airforce in time for D-Day. It was designed using the Hawker Typhoon as a template but was intended as a more potent air-to-air fighter than its predecessor. However, by the time it entered widespread service, the Luftwaffe was very much a declining force and the Tempest found a role in combating the V1 rockets in the final stages of the war.

At present only one complete Tempest is on display in the UK. It is currently housed at the London site of the RAF Museum. NV778 was too late for active service and spent its operational life towing targets for air-to-air gunnery practice, a hazardous occupation, hence the bright colour scheme. There is promise of more Hawker Tempests being on display soon; the RAF Museum, which is the proud owner of this aircraft, is currently restoring another one. There is also an ongoing restoration project at Sywell Aerodrome, in Northamptonshire, where Air Leasing is hoping to see a Tempest take to the air very soon. Finally, the South Yorkshire Aviation Museum owns a cockpit section that is slowly being developed into a larger exhibit.

CHAPTER 6
LIGHT TRANSPORT AND SUPPORT AIRCRAFT

Piper L-4 Grasshopper in USMC markings, with a Westland Lysander in the background.

Not all aircraft involved in the Normandy operations performed the headline grabbing roles. There were many supporting roles behind the scenes that were essential to the war effort. Medical evacuation, liaison, transport, communication and aerial observation were all vital to the operations, but the brave pilots and crew quietly got on with their tasks without fanfare. Many of the missions were perilous and the aircraft often outdated or hastily converted to a role for which they were not designed. The light aircraft available for these roles rarely had armour, speed or weapons, leaving them extremely vulnerable to enemy defences.

The difference in aircraft design is plain to see in this image; the rugged but basic Fairchild Argus sits facing the Republic P47 Thunderbolt. The Argus with its sturdy fixed undercarriage was well-equipped for operating out of rough fields but would be no match for an enemy fighter if encountered. The more business-like Thunderbolt was considerably more powerful, faster and well-armed, making it far more suited to war. All available modern fighters were needed on the front line, leaving the lighter aircraft to fulfil the other roles behind the lines. Even the best of the fighters needed a fairly well-prepared grass-strip runway to operate.

Communication was a challenge during the Second World War. Messages via radio were easily intercepted by the enemy and much of the technology in use was experimental and in its infancy. Liaison aircraft could deliver messages more directly by ferrying important orders or transporting high commanding officers to confidential meetings. The Normandy operations were not static; once the invasion was complete, it was important to continue to move forward. Military command bases were moved from the south of England to makeshift headquarters in northern France and beyond as the invasion progressed. Small, light aircraft such as the Fairchild Argus were able to move in and out of rough airstrips to deliver messages, equipment and personnel to help establish these new bases.

Fairchild Argus III KK527 was built in 1944 as a UC-61K for the USAAF. However, it was quickly transferred to the RAF where it served until 1949. It has passed through several owners and colour schemes but appears here in British Army markings. Although its war record is unknown, aircraft like this would certainly have been on duty during the Normandy invasions and beyond.

The Avro Anson served in the RAF for over 30 years. Its sturdiness and reliability earned the aircraft the nickname *Faithful Annie*. The Avro Anson saw a varied career in the RAF. During the Battle of Britain, eight squadrons were tasked with protecting British shipping lanes. Even at this point in the war, the Ansons were beginning to show their age. Although they were steadily replaced on the front line, many were still in service well after the war. By 1943, most of the existing Ansons had been transferred to RAF Training Command to provide vital training for the mass of Dakota pilots that would be required for the invasion.

In the UK, there are a handful of Ansons on show in museums, including rare Mk Is at Duxford and the RAF Museum. There are also two airworthy Avro Anson's still flying in the UK. G-AHKX is part of the BAE Systems heritage flight and operates alongside the Shuttleworth Collection at Old Warden. This is a later development of the Anson, built for the civilian market as an Avro XIX, but it has recently been repainted to military markings and represents a post-war aircraft that was based at RAF Coningsby.

For D-Day preparations, 70 Avro Ansons were converted to carry stretchers for use as medical evacuation aircraft. These Ansons went on to support No. 271 Squadron who operated a fleet of Handley Page Harrow (known fondly as the 'Sparrow') aircraft which were purposely kitted out as aerial ambulances. The United States operated converted C-47s as their medical evacuation aircraft. These C-47s conducted the first such flight on 10 June 1944, flying out injured personnel from the 15th US Army.

Sadly, no examples of the Handley Page Harrow have survived, but the now privately owned Avro Anson WD413 pays tribute to the medical evacuation aircraft that took part in the Normandy operations. The Anson is a much later model that served with the RAF in the 1950s before being converted to passenger configuration and designated a C.21. It is now based at Sleap Aerodrome in Shropshire and currently wears D-Day markings complete with the famous black and white stripes.

Throughout the war, several clandestine missions took place. Information was vital during the planning of the invasions; high-level photo-reconnaissance could only show so much. Agents were often dropped behind enemy lines using small, improvised airstrips to quickly load and unload spies at night. The remarkable Westland Lysander had a very short take-off and landing capability, which meant it could operate comfortably on rough fields when required. As the build-up to D-Day approached, secret missions intensified in occupied France. With the help of the French Resistance, agents and ordinance were dropped into the area so that key targets such as radar installations could be attacked from the ground.

There are two airworthy Lysanders currently operating in the UK and a further two currently on static display although there are several others across the world, including a handful in Canada. Westland Lysander V9552 was originally built for the RAF but was sent to Canada in 1942 to operate as a target tug for the RCAF. Since 1999, it has been operated by the Shuttleworth Collection as V9367, a Mk III Lysander from No. 161 Squadron. The aircraft appears in its night flying markings as used by the Special Duties unit from RAF Tempsford and Tangmere between 1942 and 1945. The rasping sound of its 870hp Bristol Mercury XX engine can still be heard overhead at most of the Shuttleworth Collection's airshows throughout the summer months.

The Westland Lysander entered service in 1938 as an Army Co-operation aircraft. It was initially tasked with message dropping and artillery spotting. August 1940 saw the beginning of delivery of the newly refined Mk IIIA Lysanders. They were armed with twin guns in the rear cockpit and given self-sealing fuel tanks and an uprated Bristol Mercury air-cooled radial engine. Despite this, it was obvious that this was not going to be an aircraft suitable for the role in which it was intended. The Lysanders strengths lay elsewhere. As well as the famous clandestine missions, other Lysanders were used for search and rescue missions. Many squadrons had one on standby, ready to search for surviving aircrew forced to ditch.

Westland Lysander V9312 (G-CCOM) is owned and operated by the Aircraft Restoration Company, which spent several years painstakingly restoring it to airworthy status. It is thought to be the only true 'Westland' Lysander remaining (all others remaining have several Canadian components incorporated into their rebuilds). It was built during 1940 and served throughout the war with Nos. 613, 4 and 225 Squadrons. It is currently painted in the livery of the latter. After a landing accident in 1942 it was sent to Canada for target tug duties where it remained until 1946. RAF and RCAF pilots would have benefitted from its services as they prepared for their part in the invasion.

Another multi-purpose aircraft used during the period was the Beechcraft Model 18, sometimes known as the Beech 18, UC-45 Expeditor or simply the Twin Beech. Over 4,500 Beech 18s were used in military service between 1937 and the late 1960s. It was a versatile aircraft capable of many roles. During 1944 it was used as a light transport, aircrew trainer, photo-reconnaissance platform and a target tug. The popular aircraft was exported all over the world and adopted for military and civilian use. It was capable of over 200mph and could easily carry six passengers.

There are several surviving Beechcraft 18s across the world, most of which are based in America. There is one on display in the UK at the National Museum of Flight in Scotland and two airworthy wartime examples are regularly seen in the skies over the UK; G-BKGL is currently presented in a USAAC Beech C-45 1164 military colour scheme, which very recently had D-Day stripes added. The other example is owned by Carlo Ferrari, registered in the US and based in Switzerland. This Beech G18S often tours UK airshows and has appeared in many films and TV shows including the recent *Catch-22* TV series. It is pictured above wearing its *Catch-22* livery.

Some of the most unsung D-Day aircraft were those that were tasked to perform in the dangerous Air Observation Post (AOP) role. These aircraft provided vital support to the land- and sea-based forces. They would fly high over the battleground and attempt to direct the artillery fire in the right direction. They were also tasked with counter-battery work, photo-reconnaissance and communications. German officers found them to be one of the greatest problems of the battle; they usually flew just beyond the range of the German infantry weapons as they calmly directed the Allies' fire.

Many Taylorcraft Auster AOPs are still flying today, but earlier marks are quite rare. NX534 is an example of a Mk IIIe variant that was built in 1943 and served with the RAF during the war. It is currently adorned with the famous invasion stripes of D-Day and is still airworthy. The Auster Mk IIIe was essentially the same as the Auster Mk I but fitted with the famous de Havilland Gipsy Major engine.

Auster Mk V TJ569 displayed at the Army Flying Museum in Middle Wallop.

Auster Mk V TJ534.

Initially the Auster squadrons were collected under Army Co-operation Command, but as plans were underway for the invasion this was disbanded, and its assets were transferred to the Second Tactical Air Force on 31 March 1943. The first British Auster AOP squadron arrived in France just two days after D-Day. It would be joined by another five squadrons within the next few weeks.

During the Second World War, there were several variants of the Auster in service. The Mks III, IV and V were the most dominant types in service throughout 1944. The Auster V became the most numerous variant of all and benefitted from armour plating, improved flaps and blind-flying instruments. Like the Mk IV, it was refitted with the American Lycoming engine instead of the de Havilland Gipsy Major. The large wing area gave the aircraft a low stall speed making it capable of landing on rough and short airstrips, perfect for recolonising the makeshift airfields in northern France shortly after the invasion.

The American's first choice in the AOP role was the L-4 Grasshopper. Around 350 of these were deployed to France immediately after the troops had landed. Many were flown in over the English Channel, whilst others were stripped down and shipped to their locations in crates. Not all the aircraft survived this hazardous journey, many were unpacked to reveal bullet holes sustained when landing on the beaches.

L-4H Grasshopper 43-29282 was built in 1943 and taken on charge with the USAAF later that year. It remains airworthy and is based in the UK. It is seen here on approach to Halfpenny Green Airfield near Wolverhampton.

The Piper L-4 Grasshopper was developed for the military from the popular light civilian aircraft, the Piper Cub. The 'L' stands for liaison aircraft and they were used for scouting, delivery of mail and movement of personnel behind enemy lines, in addition to the dangerous AOP role. Originally, the pilot sat in the front seat with the observer sitting on a sling facing backwards so that he could look out of the extended windows, although this was later abandoned. Light aircraft such as the Grasshopper and Auster were able to locate and target enemy forces beyond the visual range of ground-based observers.

The simple design, and relatively low running cost of the aircraft, has made it one of the most popular warbirds flown in civilian hands today; numerous Grasshoppers survive today. L-4B Grasshopper 43-1145 entered service in 1944 with the Free French Air Force in North Africa and moved with them to Italy following the successful Allied invasion. After the war, 43-1145 was put to civilian use in France until 1973 when it was brought to the UK by Biggin Hill Shipping and Airlines Ltd. Along with the other unique aircraft operated by Shipping and Airlines Ltd, the L-4B is a regular attendee at UK airshows throughout the summer months.

The Piper J-3 Cub has a simple, lightweight design which gives it good low-speed handling properties and short-field performance, which made it ideal for adaption to military service as the L-4 Grasshopper. In June 1944, the L-4's slow cruising speed made it an ideal observation platform for searching the hedgerows and undergrowth for hidden German artillery. The crew of two were often required to carry a large radio that exceeded the safe operational weight limits of the aircraft. As the war progressed, some L-4s were even equipped with bazooka rocket launchers to launch improvised ground attacks if required.

L-4J Grasshopper, G-BHVV, is painted to represent the United States Marine Corp (USMC) aircraft 42-38384. It has been the subject of a recent restoration and is currently owned by Austrian airline pilot Thomas Kattinger. It was restored by Bygone Aviation and is presently based at Old Warden in Bedfordshire. The unusual scheme was chosen to represent the USMC Grasshoppers that were given the designation NE-1. They were predominantly based in the Pacific during the Second World War.

Shortly before they entered the war, the United States evaluated the Aeronca 65 TC Defender to see if it could fulfil light-spotting and liaison duties within the military. From this design came the Aeronca L-3 group of aircraft that were visually like the Piper variant of Grasshoppers and given the same name. Although a useful aircraft capable of performing on the front line, it was not as widespread as the Piper version and mainly saw service as a training aircraft although many did make their way to Europe during the war.

31923 G-BRHP is an example of an L-3C Aeronca Grasshopper that remains airworthy and is based in the UK. It appears regularly at events and was part of a large contingent of 'L' birds that made the trip back to Normandy for the 75th anniversary of D-Day in 2019.

CHAPTER 7

MARITIME AIRCRAFT

Consolidated PBY Catalina, operated by Plane Sailing Ltd.

At the beginning of 1944, the German Navy was still a mighty force that was not to be underestimated. The U-boats, E-boats and other surface vessels continued to pose a significant threat to both the supply lines across the Atlantic and the direct plans of a Channel-borne invasion. Coastal Command was tasked with countering this threat. Supplied with a mix of eclectic, hastily adapted, occasionally obsolescent aircraft, the often-forgotten maritime air services provided a vital contribution to the D-Day operations.

The popular Fly Navy Airshow at the Shuttleworth Collection often provided a superb mix of maritime aircraft; here is an unusual flypast of Second World War maritime aircraft consisting of the Gloster Gladiator, Fairey Swordfish and North American Harvard.

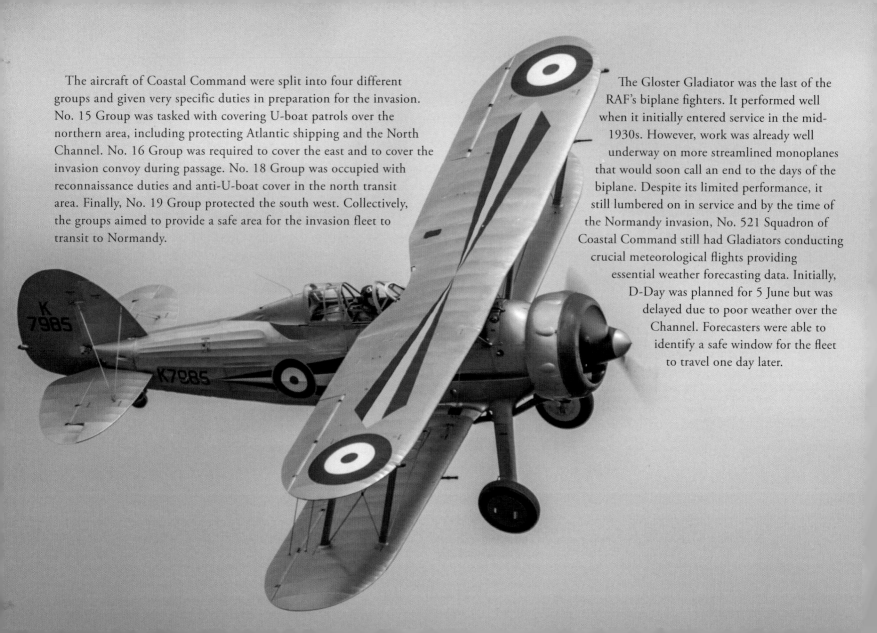

The aircraft of Coastal Command were split into four different groups and given very specific duties in preparation for the invasion. No. 15 Group was tasked with covering U-boat patrols over the northern area, including protecting Atlantic shipping and the North Channel. No. 16 Group was required to cover the east and to cover the invasion convoy during passage. No. 18 Group was occupied with reconnaissance duties and anti-U-boat cover in the north transit area. Finally, No. 19 Group protected the south west. Collectively, the groups aimed to provide a safe area for the invasion fleet to transit to Normandy.

The Gloster Gladiator was the last of the RAF's biplane fighters. It performed well when it initially entered service in the mid-1930s. However, work was already well underway on more streamlined monoplanes that would soon call an end to the days of the biplane. Despite its limited performance, it still lumbered on in service and by the time of the Normandy invasion, No. 521 Squadron of Coastal Command still had Gladiators conducting crucial meteorological flights providing essential weather forecasting data. Initially, D-Day was planned for 5 June but was delayed due to poor weather over the Channel. Forecasters were able to identify a safe window for the fleet to travel one day later.

During May 1944, the Germans decided to move their U-boats from Norway down to the Bay of Biscay. RAF Coastal Command attempted to stop the move before it happened. They sent reinforcements to the bases in Scotland to counter the movements. The operations were not without loss for the Allies, but over 51 German submarines were attacked, of which 28 were sunk or damaged. The Consolidated PBY Catalina was considered the best tool for anti-U-boat missions; it was operated by both the RAF and USAAF.

Several Catalinas have survived, and, incredibly, a few were still operating as aerial firefighting units well into the 21st century. Only two complete examples are on show in the United Kingdom, one of which is airworthy. The RAF Museum hosts this Catalina in Royal Danish Air Force colours at their Cosford site.

The Consolidated PBY is universally known now as the Catalina, based on its British designation during the Second World War. It was built in greater numbers than any other flying boat and remained in production for over ten years. The Catalina was a surprisingly slow aircraft with a maximum speed of just 200mph; it was slow even for a flying boat of that time. It was not its speed but its range, payload and reliability that made this aircraft so good at its job.

G-PBYA is currently based at Duxford and is owned and operated by Plane Sailing. It is a regular performer at airshows in the UK and Europe. G-PBYA was originally ordered for the RCAF, built as a PBY-5A.

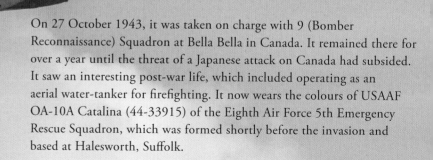

On 27 October 1943, it was taken on charge with 9 (Bomber Reconnaissance) Squadron at Bella Bella in Canada. It remained there for over a year until the threat of a Japanese attack on Canada had subsided. It saw an interesting post-war life, which included operating as an aerial water-tanker for firefighting. It now wears the colours of USAAF OA-10A Catalina (44-33915) of the Eighth Air Force 5th Emergency Rescue Squadron, which was formed shortly before the invasion and based at Halesworth, Suffolk.

Consolidated PBY Catalina G-PBYA at sunrise.

The Catalina would typically carry a crew of nine on its long missions; its later variants could fly for over 3,500 miles before refuelling. Catalinas were used for a variety of roles including search and rescue, reconnaissance and bombing. The aircraft would typically be armed with two forward-facing machine guns, one on each side, and another capable of firing to the rear. It could also carry a range of bombs and depth charges; many variants were even fitted with onboard radar systems.

The Canadian, Australian, US and British forces all operated Catalinas in great numbers. RAF Coastal Command and the US Navy were the biggest users of Catalinas, and they were operational for most of the war. The PBY Catalina was built at factories in the US and Canada as well as under licence in the Soviet Union. It operated in every theatre of the Second World War and was widely used for anti-submarine warfare, maritime patrol, search and rescue and reconnaissance.

The Consolidated PBY Catalina's considerable range and large crew gave it a real advantage when searching for the elusive German submarines. On 24 May 1944, a Catalina of No. 210 Squadron claimed victory over German U-boat *U-476*. Despite the U-boat returning considerable anti-aircraft fire, the Catalina was able to drop six depth charges on the target. The final depth charge did not manage a direct hit, but it was close enough to flip and damage the U-boat, causing it to slowly sink.

G-PBYA wears the colours of the USAAF search and rescue unit. The USAAF had used Catalinas for air and sea rescue work in the Mediterranean but had relied on RAF aircraft for rescues around the UK. Shortly before the planned invasion, General Spaatz ordered some of his own Catalinas to join the northern European operations. By the end of 1944, the Eighth Air Force 5th Emergency Rescue Squadron was fully operational with Catalinas. Plane Sailing's airworthy Catalina pays tribute to these operations.

The enormous Short Sunderland flying boat was nicknamed the 'Flying Porcupine' by the Germans due to its impressive defensive armament. During the invasion, the huge flying boats were almost constantly out, undertaking long missions in often challenging conditions. Despite its lumbering size, the Sunderland was a surprisingly effective foe against the Luftwaffe aircraft that they would often encounter on U-boat patrols. It was one of the most powerful and widely-used flying boats throughout the Second World War

On 2 June 1943, eight Junkers Ju 88Cs attacked a single Sunderland Mk III of No. 461 (RAAF) Squadron.

The Sunderland boat proved its worth and was able to shoot down three of the Ju 88s before lumbering 350 miles home to beach itself near Cornwall. All ten aircrew survived the incident. RAF Coastal Command operated five squadrons of Sunderlands during the Normandy invasions; the Royal Australian Air Force (RAAF) made up the sixth squadron that was in operation over Europe at the time. There are two complete Short Sunderlands on display in the UK: one in the RAF Museum at Hendon, and the other (pictured here) is on display at the IWM in Duxford.

led to an aircraft that would play a major part in bombing and reconnaissance until the four-engine heavies took over duties in the middle of the war. By the time of the Normandy invasion, Wellingtons had all been transferred to Coastal Command and were mainly playing supporting roles rather than frontline bombing.

Wellington bombers were often called upon to support night operations during the Normandy invasions. They were tasked with dropping flares to act as pathfinders for other units. Wellington MF628 is a T.10 variant that is currently in a stripped-down state but will soon be returned to display in the RAF Museum. It is one of only two complete surviving Wellingtons in the UK. This Wellington is known to have flown on a mission on 3 June 1944, although the purpose of this flight is unclear. The aircraft was moved into long-term storage shortly afterwards.

The Vickers Wellington was designed by Dr Barnes Wallis (of bouncing bomb Dambusters fame). The prototype made its first flight on 15 June 1936. During the early stages of the war, the Wellington did not fare well against German fighters. Many modifications including additional protection, self-sealing fuel tanks and redesigned hydraulics

The threat the German Navy posed to the success of Operation *Overlord* cannot be understated. On D-Day itself and the days following the invasion, Coastal Command were given the task of protecting the shipping lanes into Normandy. The eclectic fleet of aircraft were on constant patrols in search of U-boats and other German shipping that could have seriously disrupted the invasion plans. The maritime aircraft were very successful at protecting the funnel in which the Allied ships travelled. Very few ships were lost en route to Normandy in June 1944, but 23 aircraft from Coastal Command would be destroyed protecting them.

The Grumman Wildcat was an American carrier-based fighter aircraft that began service in 1940 with the United States Navy and the British Fleet Air Arm (FAA). Initially it was known as the Martlet in British service, but by January 1944, the FAA reverted to its American name. The Royal Navy had over 1,200 Wildcats in service throughout the war; they were even part of the very last air raid of the Second World War.

Grumman Wildcat FM2 G-RUMW was built in 1945 for the US Navy by General Motors. It entered service just as the war had finished so was placed in storage until being transferred to civilian ownership in 1946. It is now owned and operated by the Fighter Collection at the IWM Duxford. It currently wears the scheme of FAA Wildcats that were on board HMS *Tracker* in 1944. In April 1944, the aircraft from HMS *Tracker* were responsible for the sinking of the German U-boat *U-288*, just off the coast of Norway.

The Royal Navy, however, operated three squadrons during the time of the Normandy invasion.

Grumman Avengers were often deployed on aircraft carriers alongside Wildcats that would provide fighter cover for the Avengers torpedo attacks. HMS *Tracker* operated both aircraft types in support of the D-Day landings, providing a submarine screen for the invasion fleet. With so many Allied ships in the water, a collision seemed inevitable and such was the fate of HMS *Tracker* on 10 June 1944 when it hit a Canadian ship. Fortunately, damage was minor, and the *Tracker* was able to limp home for repairs.

Although there are numerous Avengers surviving in the US, only two are currently on display in the UK: one is at the FAA Museum in Yeovilton; the other (pictured here) is on display at the IWM in Duxford. Duxford's Avenger is currently painted in the markings of an aircraft flown by former US president George Bush, who served in the war with the Pacific fleet. It was built in 1944 and supplied to the Canadian Navy and passed through several post-war civilian hands before arriving at Duxford in 1977.

Another Grumman aircraft designed for the US Navy in operation at the time was the Grumman TBF Avenger. Like the Wildcat, this aircraft was also adopted by the Royal Navy as a carrier-based torpedo bomber. The Avenger was the most effective and widely-used torpedo bomber of the Second World War, but in US hands it was mostly deployed in the Pacific.

The Hawker Hurricane was much loved by its pilots. It was praised for its fire power and its ability to absorb punishment. It was the true work horse of the Battle of Britain, but by 1944 it was no longer an effective frontline fighting aircraft. However, the naval variant of the popular fighter the Sea Hurricane was still in limited service by D-Day. Although still a nimble fighter, the lack of folding wings and its large airframe proved cumbersome for deck operations. The last unit operating the Sea Hurricane was No. 835 Squadron, which converted to Wildcats in September 1944.

The Supermarine Spitfire and Hawker Hurricane had proved so effective in the early stages of the war that naval versions of both aircraft were immediately tested. In fact, the idea of a maritime Spitfire had been suggested as early as 1938, but, wisely, it was decided that all efforts be put into land-based Spitfire production for the time being. After the Battle of Britain, the concept was discussed again which eventually led to the first Seafires entering service towards the end of 1942.

The Hawker Hurricane's history can be traced back to the Hawker biplane fighters of the 1930s. Sydney Camm, Hawker's chief designer since 1925, had already developed successful biplane fighters for the RAF but felt he had maximised the potential that a biplane could offer. An advancement in technology meant that losing the top wing, which was hitherto essential for structural support, was now a reality and the potential of the monoplane could be unlocked. Although not as adaptable as the Spitfire, the Sea Hurricane was successful during the middle stages of the war before being phased out for more suitable carrier-based aircraft.

The Shuttleworth Collection's Sea Hurricane forms up with Air Leasing's Supermarine Seafire.

From November 1942, the Supermarine Seafire saw service with the Royal Navy's FAA. It played a major part in the North African and Italian Allied invasions and was also tasked with providing aerial support on D-Day. By this time, the Seafire Mk III was the dominant variant. It was the first fully adapted maritime version of the Spitfire complete with folding wings and a specialised air filter system for the harsh sea air.

There have been two airworthy Seafires operating in the UK over the last few years although both have been grounded recently. Air Leasing based at Sywell in Northamptonshire operates PP972 (G-BUAR) a low-flying (LF) Mk III variant. Whilst Seafire F. XVII SX336 is an example of a later Griffon-powered variant that served after the Second World War, currently owned by Kennet Aviation. Both British Seafires should be back in action soon following major repair and servicing works.

It seems incredible that a large open cockpit biplane was still in service during the Allied D-Day invasion, but the Fairey Swordfish is a real survivor. Having already found fame for its role in the sinking of the German Battleship the *Bismarck* in 1941, the Swordfish torpedo bomber had nothing left to prove. However, despite its ageing design there were still three squadrons of them in service at the time of the Normandy invasion.

W5856 is the oldest surviving airworthy Fairey Swordfish in the world. It was built in October 1941 by Blackburn aircraft and therefore known as a Blackfish. W5856 saw service in the middle part of the Second World War in the Mediterranean theatre, but by 1944 it was relegated to training duties in Canada. The aircraft took its first post-restoration flight in 2015 and currently wears the colours of No. 820 Naval Air Squadron, as worn during the attack of the *Bismarck* in 1941. It is one of three Swordfish operated under the Navy Wings banner. It is hoped they will all be made airworthy in time.

Many Swordfish aircraft were operated at night, undertaking anti-shipping strikes with support from other aircraft such as Wellington bombers, which would use flares to light up targets. The Swordfish was also produced as a floatplane, which proved useful from D-Day onwards where it was deployed close to the beaches to direct ship-to-shore bombardments. The legendary flexibility of the machine was further proven when it was required to lay smoke screens to cover the invasion fleet shortly before landing on the beaches of Normandy.

For night operations, the Fairey Swordfish was given an all-black matt finish to aid camouflage in the dark skies. This look can be seen on the Swordfish on display at the IWM Duxford. NF370 is a Mk III Swordfish that entered FAA service on April Fools' day in 1944. On the underside of this aircraft you can see the casing for a large radar unit which would have aided the perilous night patrols.

Bristol Beaufighter RD253 at the RAF Museum in Hendon.

The Fighter Collection's Bristol Beaufighter JM135 is currently under restoration.

Bristol Beaufighters started to arrive in the RAF by August 1940 with the first operational sorties taking place on 18 September. The twin-engine aircraft was conceived as a fighter but did not prove successful in this role. Although not the perfect fighter, the Beaufighter did go on to serve with distinction in many roles throughout the war, finding its niche in long-range missions for Coastal Command. The Bristol Beaufighter was also considered ideal for attacking surface vessels including both merchant and military targets during the build-up to the invasion. A unit of Beaufighters was also reserved to carry out dawn and dusk sweeps looking for light enemy crafts as they were entering or leaving the harbours.

There are three Beaufighters on display in the UK. One can be seen at the RAF Museum in Hendon. Although it did not enter service until October 1944, it is currently displayed as a D-Day Beaufighter. The Fighter Collection at Duxford is currently undertaking a complex restoration of this aircraft, which is still awaiting suitable Bristol Hercules engines to power the aircraft back to the skies. The other UK Beaufighter is on display at the National Museum of Flight near Edinburgh.

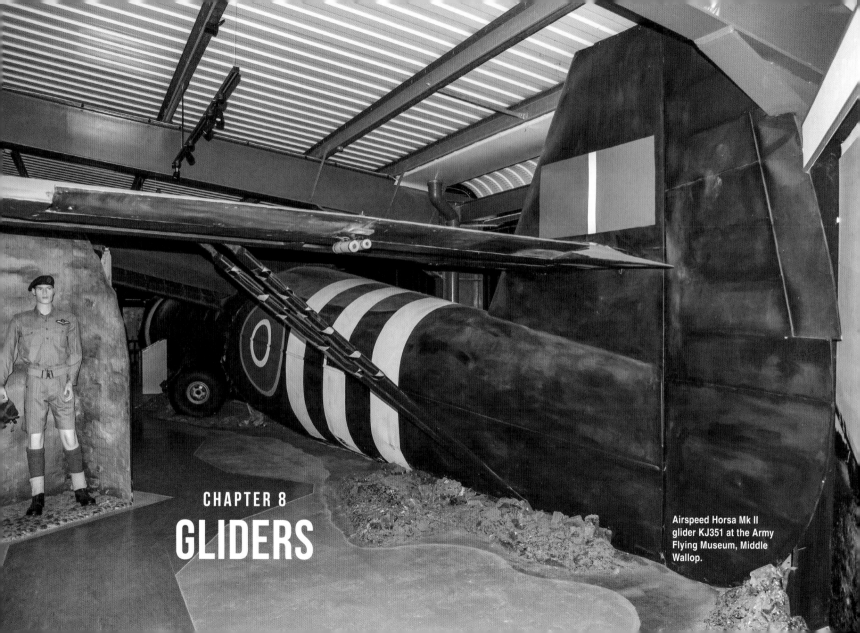

CHAPTER 8
GLIDERS

Airspeed Horsa Mk II glider KJ351 at the Army Flying Museum, Middle Wallop.

In the early hours of 6 June 1944, ahead of the main invasion fleet, thousands of British and American troops were dropped behind enemy lines to seize key locations such as the now-famous Pegasus Bridge. To get the troops and equipment into position, an audacious airborne assault was conceived. Large wooden gliders carrying troops, vehicles and artillery would be tugged into position by large transport aircraft such as the Albemarle, Halifax, Sterling and Dakota, before being released to land in the fields of northern France. The gliders would be followed by thousands of paratroopers laden with heavy equipment, all attempting to land safely in unknown territory in total darkness.

There would be no second chances for the glider-borne force. They would be flying without an engine and too low for parachutes. The pilots had to get the landing right first time, a tall order when making their approach to unknown, unprepared fields in total darkness. To add to the problem, the landing zones were often sprinkled with anti-glider landing obstacles that became known as 'Rommel's asparagus'. It was a truly dangerous undertaking even before arriving at the battle; no wonder the wooden, unpowered aircraft became known as 'flying coffins'.

Germany was the first nation to attempt a glider-based assault. Having been effectively restricted from forming an air force in the Treaty of Versailles, German officials needed to find a subtle solution to re-arming the nation. They encouraged the production of gliders such as the Schneider Grunau Baby (pictured here) which were then employed to train their pilots before they had access to powered aircraft.

This experience with glider production gave German military leaders other ideas. During the invasion of Belgium in 1940, the glider-borne paratroopers of Flieger-Division landed on the roof of the Eben-Emael fortress on the Belgium border. It was previously thought to be impregnable. After successfully laying explosives around the fortress, the small German force were able to take the fortress by complete surprise. Ironically, after heavy losses, Hitler did not pursue the idea of glider assaults any further during the war.

The idea of an airborne glider assault was noted by Prime Minster Winston Churchill who even before the end of the Battle of Britain had set about motions to form a glider training school. By September 1940, the Glider Training Squadron was operational, although the production of purpose-built training gliders lagged slightly. An appeal was made for civilian gliders to be donated to the squadron. The first four arrived in August 1941. Ironically, three of these gliders were made in Germany before the war.

The Schneider SG38 was a popular glider in use in Germany before the war. Although a very basic design, its high wing and simplicity made it suitable for first flight training. The Shuttleworth Collection still flies a glider of this design. It was built after the war by Elliotts of Newbury (EoN) and became known as the EoN primary glider. It represents the type of glider that many Luftwaffe pilots would have had their first solo flight in, and was also adopted by British glider pilot training, with cadets using it well after the war.

In 1935, Fred Slingsby who owned a woodworking factory in Scarborough set about redesigning the German Grunau Baby, which he was already building under licence. He replaced the fuselage with a more streamlined structure and removed the straight wings in favour of a gull-shaped wing. The resulting prototype became a success at the British Gliding Association Championships that year. When the war broke out, these gliders were amongst the first acquisitioned for the No. 1 Glider Training Squadron at Haddenham.

This particular example was built in 1937 by Slingsby Sailplanes Ltd. It was extensively rebuilt in the 1980s and in 2011, it became part of the Shuttleworth Collection, where it still flies today.

An unusual use of the Slingsby Kite was as a test for British radar. After the glider assault over Belgium, and the knowledge that the German forces had several gliders on strength, it seemed logical to expect a glider-based invasion of England. As such, several Kites from the Glider Pilot Regiment at Haddenham near Thame were adapted to test the limits of British radar. As many metal components as possible were removed, even the cables were replaced with oak pushrods. These aircraft became known as the Radar Kite – incredibly, the one pictured here is still flying today.

With only limited capacity on troop-carrying transports, paratrooper drops were usually limited to around 20 soldiers at a time. It quickly became clear that getting larger forces into France would require a significant glider force. On 21 December 1941, the Glider Pilot Regiment was formed. Its pilots would be made up of Army volunteers trained by the RAF. Army volunteers would enter the Elementary Flying Training School and learn how to fly on a de Havilland Tiger Moth before progressing to a Miles Magister. Once powered flight had been mastered, they would be given the GAL.48 Hotspur to hone their skills as an assault glider pilot.

The Miles Aircraft company developed the Magister from its civilian Hawk Major and Hawk Trainer. It proved a step up from the Tiger Moth but retained the fixed undercarriage and open cockpit; it was also powered by a Gipsy Major. This Magister was registered as V1075 in the RAF where it served until 1942. It is now owned by one of the Shuttleworth Collection's pilots, David Bramwell. The Tiger Moth pictured belongs to the Classic Wings fleet at Duxford.

General Aircraft Ltd was issued a Ministry of Aircraft Production contract to produce a glider for the airborne establishment. It came up with the General Aircraft GAL.48 Hotspur. It was the first glider purposely produced with an assault in mind although it could only carry up to eight troops at a time. Very soon, bigger, more efficient gliders were produced and most of the Hotspurs were transferred to training units. An evaluation was undertaken in Canada to explore the possibility of Supermarine Spitfires towing the glider into battle, but, ultimately, no Hotspur would be used on the front line.

The Hotspur exhibited excellent flying characteristics and could be used for aerobatics. Novice pilots found it easy to master after their initial flight training experiences. Ballasts were used to balance the aircraft during training as no troops were on board. Novice pilots were also expected to practise night flying before being declared operational. HH368 is a replica Hotspur currently on display at the Army Flying Museum at Middle Wallop, Hampshire. The only other example in the UK is a cockpit section on display at the Dumfries and Galloway Aviation Museum in Scotland.

Another training aircraft widely used by the RAF was the Slingsby T.21. It entered service in 1944 in a response to the growing demand for glider pilots. It is a scaled-up development of the single-seat German Grunau Baby, with a slightly larger fuselage and side-by-side cockpit. Up until this point, glider training had mostly been a solo affair. Introduction of this type of glider greatly reduced the accident rate: having an experienced pilot at your side could be a lifesaver for new pilots.

The Slingsby T.21 became known as the Sedbergh in RAF service although its introduction would have been a little too late to have a major impact on the D-Day preparations. However, the experiences gained from training for Normandy set the pattern for training new pilots in the British forces for a long time to come. The Slingsby Sedbergh was so well designed that it remained in operation until it was replaced by the Viking glider in the 1980s.

The Airspeed Horsa was taken from a drawing board concept to first flight in little over ten months. Airspeed Ltd was a subsidiary company to de Havilland aircraft and as such the design team at Salisbury Hall, under the direction of lead designer, A E Ellison, produced the prototype which took its first successful flight on 12 September 1941. The Horsa was characterised by its high long wings and cylindrical fuselage that could carry heavy equipment, vehicles or up to 25 troops.

In the rush to build up an invasion fleet, Horsa production was subcontracted out to several companies. As most aircraft firms were tied up with production of core powered aircraft, wooden glider production was left to companies specialising in woodwork such as furniture, cabinet and piano makers. The result was the production of almost 4,000 Horsa gliders which would be used by both the British and American forces. Today, only a handful of these gliders survive. This Airspeed Horsa cockpit can be found in the impressive Airborne Assault Museum at Duxford.

Large numbers of Horsas were subsequently used during the opening stages of the Battle of Normandy, and took part in the British Operation *Tonga* and American operations. The Horsa could carry 25 troops plus a crew of two, who in British hands were also trained soldiers. Alternatively, the Horsa could also carry a six-pound gun including its crew and tow jeep. The glider had a maximum gliding speed of 100mph making it an easy target for ground artillery, which often encouraged pilots to make hasty landings.

The Army Flying Museum in Hampshire is fortunate to have examples of all the D-Day gliders in its collection including this Airspeed Horsa. KJ351 is a Horsa Mk II glider and an almost complete survivor, which is rare. The museum also holds the substantial remains of two other Airspeed Horsa Mk IIs.

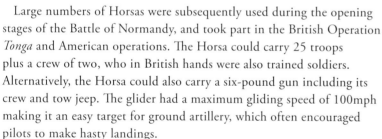

After completion of the Airspeed Horsa Mk I, the design team moved to Portsmouth to work on the Mk II. This improved variant featured a hinged nose which would allow vehicles and large artillery to be loaded and unloaded onto the glider. On the battlefield, the glider's rear fuselage could be quickly detached by detonating a small charge to blow it apart quickly. If time permitted, the tail section could be removed more carefully with a spanner.

Landing accidents were common with the glider and, if required, the main undercarriage could be jettisoned to allow landing on a central sprung skid. Trials with a brake chute were also undertaken, but the glider travelled too slowly for these to open effectively. It was left to the pilot's daring and skill to get the aircraft down as quickly and safely as possible.

Another example of the Mk II Horsa at the Army Flying Museum in Middle Wallop shows the additional access that could be gained by removing the cockpit section of the aircraft.

The Army Flying Museum's Waco Glider.

Unlike the British, the US trained specialist pilots who were not trained to fight on the ground as well; their only responsibility was to get the glider to the landing zone safely and unload.

Although the US had over 300 Horsa gliders at their disposal, their preferred choice was the US-designed Waco CG-4A glider. Almost 14,000 Wacos were produced using the skills and materials of the Michigan state furniture industry to great effect. The Waco was known as the Hadrian in RAF service and could carry 15 troops or almost 18,000lbs of equipment. It was smaller than the Horsa with a slower descent speed which made for softer landings but a more vulnerable target.

In the United States, the concept of airborne units was not popular with military commanders. President Franklin Roosevelt was the first to spearhead the movement and formed the first paratrooper platoon in 1940, but it was not until 1942 that this became a major part of the force when it was split into two divisions. One of them was a glider infantry regiment.

Gliders were often designed with a one-way trip in mind. The objective was to get the troops and equipment into battle as quickly as possible. This, added to their significantly wooden structure, has meant that few examples of any Second World War gliders have survived. Only the Yorkshire Air Museum and the Army Flying Museum have Waco CG-4As in their collections within the UK.

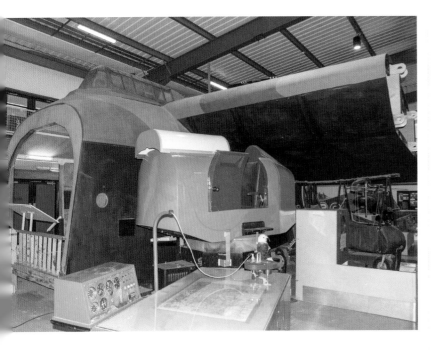

The General Aircraft Hamilcar was the largest of the Allied gliders operating on D-Day. In fact, it remains the largest wooden aircraft ever constructed. Fewer than 400 Hamilcars were built, most of them by subcontractors such as the Birmingham Railway Carriage & Wagon Company. Because of the aircraft's huge weight, only the Handley Page Halifax was effectively able to tow it on operations. It was designed to carry large equipment and vehicles into action. In effect, it was the only glider that could safely deliver tanks into battle, which could be unloaded in just 15 seconds if required.

Hamilcars were only used on three occasions. Their first operations were for the Normandy landings when approximately 30 were used to carry anti-tank guns, transport vehicles and Tetrarch light tanks to equip the British troops. Following the immediate invasion, Hamilcars could also carry equipment required to construct a makeshift airfield, including a HD10 bulldozer if deconstructed and split across three gliders. The Army Flying Museum has two segments of General Aircraft Ltd Hamilcars on display including this replica front section.

CHAPTER 9
DOUGLAS DAKOTAS/C-47/C-53

Two of the UK-based Douglas C-47 Skytrains, *Drag em oot* and *Aces High*, in formation.

Shortly before midnight on 5 June 1944, all was ready for the start of the huge airborne assault on Normandy. The British forces were spilt into three airborne operations: *Tonga, Mallard* and *Rob Roy*. For operation *Tonga*, six Albemarles took off carrying the troops of the 22nd Independent Parachute Company. Their task was to set up Eureka homing beacons and lights on the drop zones to guide the forces into position. Shortly afterwards, 71 Dakotas and four Albemarles transported the primary force carrying the 3rd Parachute Brigade. Their targets included taking control over key bridges to prevent any German troop movements.

The Douglas Dakota entered RAF service in March 1943. It was essentially the same aircraft as the C-47 Skytrain, which had been in service for the USAAF for over a year. It marked a turning point for the RAF, as it was the first purpose-built transport aircraft (most of the RAF's other transport aircraft to this point were simply adapted bombers). Dakota C Mk III ZA947 is now the only Dakota that remains in RAF service, making up a key element of the BBMF.

Operation *Mallard* was the immediate follow-up to the first wave and saw a risky daylight landing in enemy territory just behind the main land-based beach invasion. The British forces launched a huge wave of aircraft including over 70 Dakotas towing Horsa gliders. Short Stirlings and Albemarles also pulled Horsa and Hamilcar gliders into position. The objective was to cut off the anticipated German counter-attack. The landings were largely successful, but one Dakota was shot down en route.

The RAF has operated almost 2,000 Dakotas throughout its history. ZA947 is now the only one left. It was built at Long Beach, California in 1943 and served during the war in Canada for the RCAF. It proved itself in extreme weather conditions operating around Newfoundland and Goose Bay. It served for the RCAF until 1969. It was then transferred to the Royal Aircraft Establishment at Farnborough in the UK for duties in its test flight fleet. It eventually joined the BBMF in 1998. It was originally planned to operate as the support aircraft for the flight but soon became a display aircraft in its own right.

Operation *Rob Roy* was the main British resupply mission. On the evening of D-Day, 50 Dakotas were tasked with dropping over 100 tons of supplies onto the drop zones. The Dakotas flew in Vic formations of three aircraft. In the confusion, the Dakotas experienced heavy fire from Allied shipping and the formation was required to break up. Six Dakotas were lost and only 20 per cent of them successfully reached their targets.

The BBMF's Dakota is one of the few Dakotas still flying that wears RAF markings, with the majority preferring to show the US liveries. ZA947 is currently marked up as a No. 233 Squadron aircraft from the D-Day period. It represents FZ692, which was given the famous D-Day stripes and the name *Kwicherbichen*. In June 1944, it served at RAF Blakehill Farm and flew on D-Day itself. It remained at RAF Blakehill Farm until September 1944.

The United States airborne force took off from airfields in the south of England in the early hours of D-Day, equipped with C-47 Skytrains towing Waco and Horsa gliders. The main force aimed for the west of Cherbourg and approached the drop zones on the east of the peninsula. Thick cloud and heavy flak meant that the landings and parachute drops were not as accurate as those of the British. The forces were scattered, and many were too far from the target to prove effective. A follow-up mission including over 200 gliders provided some relief later that evening.

The Douglas DC-3 was an aircraft initially designed as an airliner during the 1930s. Over 600 DC-3s were built for this purpose. As tensions were building in Europe, the US military saw potential in the design and commissioned Douglas aircraft to build military variants. These became known as the C-47 Skytrain and the C-53 Skytrooper. Over 10,000 of these were produced in the US and a further 5,000 plus were produced under licence in the Soviet Union and Japan. Remarkably, there are over 300 DC-3s still flying in the world today; a small number of these remain in commercial service.

Two C-47s *Betsy's Biscuit Bomber* and *Placid Lassie* are marked up in appropriate US markings, including invasion stripes.

The DC-3 line of aircraft is one of the most successful of all time. More than 16,000 were built and around 300 remain airworthy today. Some of these are still operating in commercial services carrying passengers, fighting fires or responding to oil spills. There are also numerous historically significant airframes on display in museums throughout the world and several operating as commemorative warbirds. There are four airworthy examples currently in the UK, but this number was boosted considerably when a number of aircraft from overseas joined the 75th anniversary of D-Day celebrations in 2019.

N341A was one of the very two aircraft requisitioned by Major General Henry 'Hap' Arnold from the DC-3 production line in 1938. It paved the way for thousands of other DC-3 types that would enter military service and is one of the only two DC-3s to be given the C-41A designation. It was set aside for VIP transport for General Arnold and other high-ranking military commanders. N341A is currently owned and operated by Golden Age Air Tours in Sonoma, California but has been travelling the world since the 75th anniversary of D-Day celebrations in 2019. It is pictured here at Duxford Aerodrome just after sunrise.

The C-47 Skytrain was the militarised version of the popular civilian airliner, the DC-3. It now featured a reinforced floor, a large port-side cargo door, basic crew seating and glider-towing gear. It could carry the majority of military kit almost anywhere. Powered by reliable Pratt & Whitney Wasp radial engines, it proved to be the perfect aircraft for transporting thousands of troops into Normandy. An aircraft so rugged and reliable that it is still going strong today.

That's All Brother was the C-47 that led over 800 aircraft into Normandy on 6 June 1944. After serving on D-Day, it went on to take part in Operations *Dragoon*, *Market Garden*, *Repulse* and *Varsity*. Incredibly, this significant airframe was left forgotten in one of America's aircraft boneyards in Wisconsin. It was recently rediscovered by historians and restored to its D-Day configuration by the Commemorative Air Force. It was returned to flight just in time to fly to Europe to mark the 75th anniversary of D-Day in 2019, where it flew across the English Channel and dropped paratroopers into France, just as it did in 1944.

The DC-3 has been known as the Gooney Bird, Dakota, Skytrain, Spooky and many other nicknames. It was produced in response to demands from the fledgling commercial air travel industry. It provided a huge technological advancement over other passenger transport available in the 1930s. The DC-3 could carry up to 21 passengers at a comfortable cruising speed almost twice as fast as its competitors. After a first flight in 1935, it was ready for its first fee-paying passengers in June 1936. It soon became the world's leading airliner.

C-47 Skytrain N74589 *Placid Lassie* was built at the Douglas Aircraft Factory in Long Beach, California. It was delivered to the USAAF in 1943 and assigned to the 74th Squadron, 434th Troop Carrier Group. At 2am on 6 June 1944, *Placid Lassie* joined 832 other C-47s carrying troops and equipment to support the pathfinding 101st Airborne Division that had already landed. Towing a Waco CG-4A glider behind, *Placid Lassie* and her comrades flew just 500ft above enemy territory before reaching the release zone, just two miles behind Utah beach. One aircraft from the squadron was lost on that mission, but over half of the gliders landed within two miles of the landing zone.

Placid Lassie also took part in every major campaign of the Second World War after D-Day, before passing through several civilian owners after the war. It is now operated by the Tunison Foundation in the United States. *Placid Lassie* is still able to carry and drop paratroopers and often carries appropriately dressed re-enactors who recreate parachute drops at various events and commemorations.

Initially operating from RAF Membury during the D-Day period, N147DC flew the Heavy Glider Unit into action on that fateful day. This aircraft also served with the RAF as one of the few glider recovery aircraft that became known as 'snatchers'. In this dangerous task, the aircraft would be required to fly low over battle grounds to snag the gliders tow rope to return hardware and troops back to England.

Following the war, N147DC became involved in test flight work with Scottish Aviation, Marshals and Ferranti before joining the Royal Aircraft Establishment in 1969. Here the aircraft became known as 'Mayfly'.

There are several D-Day veteran C-47s that have survived in airworthy condition, but few have had such fascinating post-war careers as C-47 Skytrain N147DC *Mayfly*. Currently owned and operated by Aces High, this C-47 was also built at the Douglas Long Beach factory and first flew in 1943. It served with both the USAAF and the RAF.

After sterling military service, *Mayfly* entered civilian life as a film star and has appeared in over 100 productions including *Band of Brothers, Darkest Hour, Tenco, Catch-22* and *Quantum of Solace* to name but a few. In the capable ownership of Mike Woodley at Aces High, *Mayfly* is also a regular performer at UK airshows.

By the middle of the Second World War, no commercial DC-3s were being produced, instead all efforts were put into making the militarised versions. Many of the available commercial aircraft had already been converted and pressed into military service. After sterling service during the final years of the war, many surplus aircraft were converted back to civilian configurations and put into passenger services straightaway. The US forces would maintain C-47s in great numbers for a long period after the war and they were still in use for the conflict in Vietnam throughout the 1960s. At this time, many civilian aircraft were given upgraded turbo-prop engines that would allow the type to continue into the 21st century.

Although currently wearing the markings of Scandinavian Airlines, DC-3 SE-CFP *Daisy* is a veteran of the Normandy operations. *Daisy* was shipped to the USAAF in October 1943. It was initially based in Algeria but moved to England in preparation for the invasion in the spring of 1944. *Daisy* dropped the now famous (thanks to *Band of Brothers*) paratroopers of the 506th Infantry Regiment, known as Easy Company, into France on 6 June 1944. *Daisy* is currently operated by the Flying Veterans Association based in Sweden and is still licensed for parachute jumping, which the operators take every opportunity to demonstrate.

After making its first flight in July 1943, C-53 42-68830 *D-Day Doll* was delivered to the USAAF and assigned to the 72nd Troop Carrier Squadron. *D-Day Doll* is a rare D-Day surviving C-53 Skytrooper. This variant lacked the cargo door and reinforced floor that the C-47 boasted. It was a specialised troop-carrying aircraft but was not considered as versatile as the C-47 so only 380 C-53s were produced. *D-day Doll* was assigned to the 434th Troop Carrier Group at RAF Aldermaston in England and flew in every major campaign at the end of the war, including the Normandy invasion.

The aircraft has had many civilian owners since the Second World War and has operated as an airliner and cargo transport. *D-day Doll* has been owned by the Commemorative Air Force since 2001 and flies regularly at airshows in the western United States.

Although many DC-3s have remained airworthy, there are almost just as many preserved in museums in completely original and authentic condition. C-47 Skytrain 43-15509 is currently preserved at IWM Duxford. It was originally delivered to the USAAF in April 1944 and was assigned to the 316th Troop Carrier Group. It operated from RAF Cottesmore in Rutland and dropped troops over Normandy on 6 June 1944. It remained on frontline operations for the rest of the war and served as an airliner before being restored to its former glory. It is now proudly displayed hanging from the ceiling in the American Air Museum.

Presently undergoing a complex and detailed restoration at Coventry, Douglas C-47 42-100521 *Night Fright* is set to be one of the most authentic airworthy C-47s anywhere in the world. The aircraft was assigned to the 436th Troop Carrier Group of the USAAF in the very early part of 1944. Prior to D-Day, the aircraft gained the nose art and nickname *Night Fright*. It was a play on words based on one of pilot Bill Watson's favourite books: *Night Flight* by Antoine de Saint-Exupéry.

Night Fright was destined to undertake two missions over the 24-hour D-Day period. On 5 June 1944, the aircraft took off from RAF Membury at 11pm. It was carrying elements of 1st Battalion 502nd Parachute Infantry Regiment and arrived over its drop zone just after 1am on D-Day. Despite German anti-aircraft defences, the crew successfully dropped the paratroopers close to the intended location and returned home without incident.

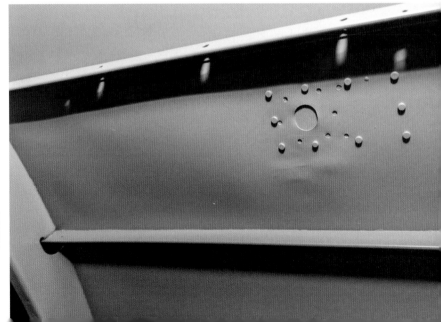

Later that evening, several C-47s including *Night Fright* and over 50 gliders departed Membury again as part of the vital resupply mission known as *Elmira*. Unfortunately, challenging conditions and German defences meant that many of the gliders were released prematurely. Some landed in or far too close to German-held territory. Despite heavy flak and a difficult return journey, all aircraft from the detail returned safely to Membury. *Night Fright* had received over 100 bullet hits that night; the repair patches of many can still be seen today.

Commercial pilot Charlie Walker and his family are the current owners of both the Membury estate and Douglas C-47 Skytrain *Night Fright*. Ambitious plans are well underway to return the aircraft to the skies and to restore the runway at Membury, with the dream of operating an authentic wartime aircraft from its original base. Every care is being taken to ensure that all elements of the aircraft are presented as it was in 1944.

to England in preparation for the Normandy invasion. On 6 June 1944, *Liberty* took off from Barkston Heath airfield towing a heavy glider and several paratroopers behind. Despite minor damage sustained during that night, the aircraft was soon back in action and served for the remainder of the war.

After the war, *Liberty* was decommissioned and sold to private hands, eventually being upgraded from a basic military freighter to a luxury airliner. In 1995, a complete restoration was undertaken, and the aircraft was given the classic 1950s polished look and a major upgrade internally. *Liberty* now boasts the latest avionics, a state-of-the-art cockpit and an ambient interior. Now in the hands of JB Air Services in Colorado, this DC-3 is possibly the most comfortable ever built.

In its striking civilian livery, it is hard to believe that DC-3C N25641 *Liberty* is also a D-Day survivor. *Liberty* began life serving the USAAF in 1943 as a C-47 with the military serial 42-32833. Initially *Liberty* was sent to serve in the African and Mediterranean theatres before being transferred

C-47A Skytrain 42-100882 is known as *Drag Em Oot*. It was delivered to the USAAF in December 1944 and assigned to the 87th Troop Carrier Squadron at Greenham Common, Berkshire. It was seen off into action on D-Day by the Allied Supreme Commander General Dwight Eisenhower. *Drag Em Oot* was also one of the 80 aircraft fitted with the glider recovery gear to be recovery gliders for future operations. It took part in the third and final assault on D-Day known as Operation *Elmira,* carrying soldiers of the 82nd Airborne Division to resupply the initial landings. In the immediate months following D-Day, *Drag Em Oot* helped to recover Waco assault gliders from the Normandy landing grounds.

Drag Em Oot was transferred to the RAF on 2 September 1944 and also served with the RCAF after the war. It still has numerous bullet holes in the cockpit and nose areas, including a bullet hole through the pilot's seat. The aircraft is now restored in 87th Squadron D-Day markings and after being based at Lincolnshire Aviation Heritage Centre for many years, *Drag Em Oot* has now been acquired by Aero Legends. You can now fly alongside this historic aircraft from out of its new base in Headcorn, Kent.

Douglas C-47 N150D was built at the Douglas Aircraft Factory in Long Beach, California in 1941. It was delivered to the USAAF on 23 June 1942 and served throughout the Second World War in Africa and the Middle East. Although not part of the Normandy landings, this aircraft still had the radio operator's and navigator's areas relatively untouched when it was recently restored. Almost all other airworthy C-47s have had these items removed over time, making this a unique, authentic example of the aircraft of that period. It now wears the D-Day markings of the 101st Airborne Division and has been given the appropriate name *Airborne Rendezvous with Destiny*.

C-47 Skytrain N62CC, *Virginia Ann* is another D-Day survivor. It was based at RAF Barkston Heath in England in 1944. Colonel Willis Mitchel chose *Virginia Ann* as the aircraft to lead the 61st Troop Carrier Group, which carried four squadrons in 72 C-47s into France on 6 June 1944. Colonel Mitchel would receive the Purple Heart for his actions that day. *Virginia Ann* would go on to serve throughout the period as a resupply and medical evacuation aircraft before going on to Operations *Market Garden* and *Varsity*. *Virginia Ann* is now operated by Mission Boston D-Day LLC in California and still wears the markings worn on 6 June 1944.

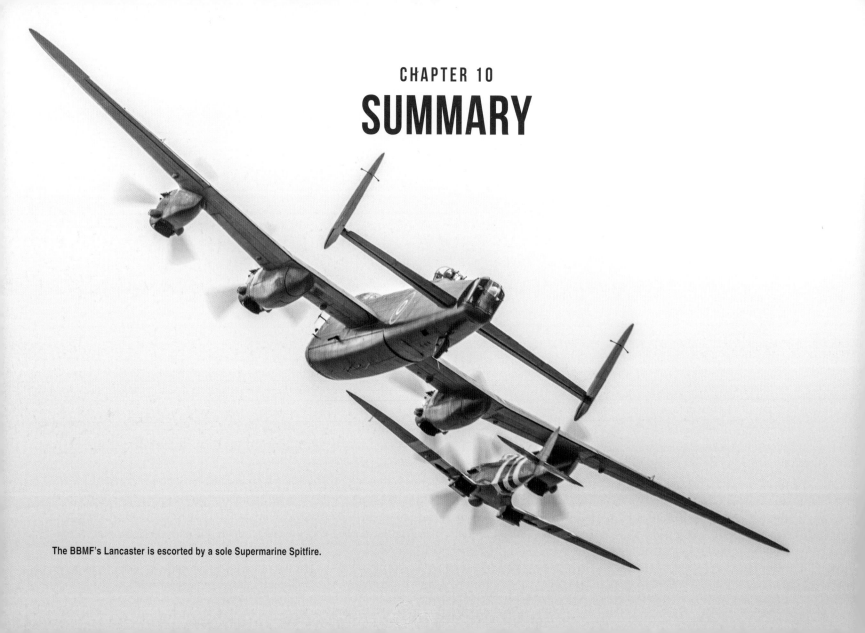

CHAPTER 10
SUMMARY

The BBMF's Lancaster is escorted by a sole Supermarine Spitfire.

By the middle of August, after almost three months of battle, the Allies had liberated Paris and the battle for Normandy was effectively over. The Allies prepared to enter Germany to meet Soviet troops advancing from the east. Although the fighting would continue at great cost, the outcome of the war now seemed inevitable. Commanders of the AEAF saw no need to let up their aerial bombardment of Germany. The bombing of German industry would continue at pace and the fighters would continue to sweep the skies until the end of the war.

The sacrifices made by all those involved will never be forgotten. Historic aircraft owners and the modern-day air forces all continue to honour those who fought for our freedom. This image shows the impressive USAF flypast for the 75th anniversary of D-Day in 2019. On the ground were four of the 23 DC-3 types that gathered to commemorate the event. In the air, six Lockheed C-130 aircraft and six Bell Boeing V-22 Ospreys of the modern transport wing made their way to Normandy via Duxford for flypasts.

P-51 Mustang *Miss Helen* whizzes over the paratroopers as they prepare to board their aircraft for a 75th anniversary paradrop in France.

Despite considerable costs, the role of the aerial forces in the success of the D-Day landings cannot be underestimated. As the land forces and aerial paratroopers approached Normandy, they met little resistance from above. The decimation of the German fighter force had been a key prerequisite of a successful invasion. It was clear by the Luftwaffe's poor showing over Normandy that this had been largely achieved. Constant bombing attacks on German airfields, radar and industry, coupled with frequent fighter sweeps, had left the Luftwaffe considerably under par.

The 75th anniversary of D-Day was widely celebrated in 2019. The airborne element of the invasion was recognised with a mass parachute drop of appropriately dressed re-enactors and a couple of veterans. In a flight of over 20 DC-3 type aircraft and a small fighter escort, the contingent had gathered from all over the world to make the journey from England to France on 5 June 2019.

The success of the diversionary tactics was also apparent. The German response to D-Day was slow and confused thanks in part to the diversionary bombing raids which included build-up attacks on the Pas-de-Calais region. Destruction of radar by aerial attacks alongside dropping of radar distraction materials known as 'chaff' or 'window' further added to the confusion.

Although named the Battle of Britain Memorial Flight, the modern-day RAF tribute flight pays homage to all those that served during the Second World War and beyond. This unique flypast of a Lancaster, Hurricane and three Spitfires was to commemorate the 75th anniversary of VJ Day in 2020. The BBMF operates two D-Day veterans including Spitfire AB910 which can be seen here with the D-Day invasion stripes.

Although the Allied air forces met little resistance from the Luftwaffe on D-Day itself, it should be noted that the work had already been done in the build-up phase. The success of countless probing missions by fighter aircraft, combined with targeted bombing raids had left the Luftwaffe in poor shape, making way for the sea and land invasion. In addition, the U-boat pens and V-rocket launch sites were also captured or rendered useless by the end of the Normandy campaign. This left most of German High Command convinced that defeat was now inevitable.

The fighter aircraft were not forgotten in the 75th anniversary of D-Day celebrations although the role of the transport aircraft such as the C-47 Skytrain dominated the events. Here we see a line-up of fighter aircraft including two Supermarine Spitfires and a Grumman Wildcat. All were given D-Day markings for the event.

Two Czech Airforce Aero L-159A Alcas form up with a Supermarine Spitfire for a brilliant past-meets-present flypast at the Cosford Airshow in 2018.

Modern-day Norwegian F16 with D-Day markings.

The well-planned co-ordination of forces in the air, at sea and on land had given the Allies a foothold in mainland Europe. The efforts started well before D-Day and would continue for almost a year afterwards, but the race to build up forces in northern France was won by the Allies. Aircraft would continue to play crucial roles in supply and transport as the lines advanced, and the fighters would need to continue their dominance in the skies to clear the way for the bombers supporting the ground forces as they marched on into Germany.

The Normandy invasion was truly a multi-nation affair. The sheer numbers of British and American forces often overshadowed the roles played by other nations, but their sacrifices are not to be forgotten. Often the modern military lead the way in these tributes.

Not all D-Day objectives were met as planned, but the airborne troops did secure the flanks and the pre-invasion aerial attacks paved the way for what turned out to be a broadly successful invasion. Although there were over 10,000 casualties, it was a mere 25 per cent of what was feared. The aerial support played a significant role in keeping this number down. D-Day is now widely considered the major turning point in the Second World War. At last the Allies were taking the fight to the enemy. In addition to the many aircraft involved, there were also around 7,000 naval vessels and around 150,000 troops involved on D-Day alone. Working as one, the multinational Allies had finally begun to put an end to tyranny.

The United States Heritage Flight also do their part in remembering the past. The newest US aircraft, the F35 Lightning II, is seen here with a Supermarine Spitfire and a P-51 Mustang.

The Royal Navy are also keen to remember their heroes; the modern-day Wildcat helicopter escorts the Fairey Swordfish in a fitting tribute.

The logistical efforts of the Normandy campaign are almost incomprehensible. It remains the largest military operation in history. The 12,000 aircraft involved on D-Day form only part of the story. Many more aircraft had helped to pave the way for the invasion: the photo-reconnaissance flights had provided up-to-date accurate data, which allowed efficient planning; the bombers had hampered German transport and industry; and the fighters had cleared the skies. On D-Day itself, the aircraft of Coastal Command had protected the fleet. The fighters provided reassurance to the landing parties, and the assault gliders and transport aircraft ensured that the troops, equipment and supplies were delivered.

The modern-day military, civilian museums and warbird owners continue to remember the sacrifices made in their own unique tributes. Although D-Day was not the end of the war, it was a significant turning point and a real cause for celebration. After four years of war, the end was clearly in sight. Many people paid with their lives for our freedom. Lest we forget.

BIBLIOGRAPHY

Addington, Scott, *Invasion! D-day & Operation Overlord in One Hundred Moments*, Unicorn Publishing (2019)

Beaver, Paul, *Spitfire Evolution*, Paul Beaver & Beaver Ltd, Westminster (2016)

Bishop, Patrick, *Fighter Boys and Bomber Boys*, Williams Collins Books, London (2017)

Blackah, Paul; Lowe, Malcolm and Blackah, Louise, *Hawker Hurricane: Owners' Workshop Manual*, Haynes Publishing, Yeovil (2010)

Chant, Chris, *Aircraft of World War II*, Amber Books (2016)

Delve, Ken, *D-Day: the Air Campaign*, Aviation History Research Centre (2019)

Dibbs, John; Holmes, Tony and Riley, Gordon, *Hurricane: Hawker's Fighter Legend*, Osprey Publishing, Oxford (2017)

Dibbs, John and Holmes, Tony, *Spitfire: The Legend Lives On*, Osprey Publishing, Oxford (2016)

Ellis, Ken, *Wrecks & Relics*, 27th Edition, Crecy Publishing (2020)

Falconer, Jonathan, *D-Day Operations Manual: Owners' Workshop Manual*, Haynes Publishing, Yeovil (2013)

Falconer, Jonathan, *RAF Bomber Command: Owners' Workshop Manual*, Haynes Publishing, Yeovil (2018)

Freeman, Roger, A., *American Air Museum Duxford*, Midland Publishing (2001)

Hastings, Max, *Chastise: The Dambusters*, Williams Collins Books, London (2019)

Holland, James, *Normandy '44: D-Day and the Battle for France*, Bantam Press (2019)

Holmes, Tony (editor), *Dogfight: The greatest air duels of World War II*, Osprey Publishing, Oxford (2011)

Humberstone, Jim, *Fairey Swordfish: Owners' Workshop Manual*, Haynes Publishing, Yoevil (2014)

Mckay, Sinclair, *The Secret Life of Fighter Command: The men and women who beat the Luftwaffe*, Autumn Press, London (2015)

Nichol, John, *Spitfire*, Simon & Schuster UK Ltd, London (2018)

Price, Alfred and Blackah, Paul, *Supermarine Spitfire: Owners' Workshop Manual*, Haynes Publishing, Yeovil (2007)

Riley, Gordon, *Hawker Hurricane Survivors*, Grub Street, London (2015)

Wilson, Keith, *Battle of Britain Memorial Flight: Operations Manual*, Haynes Publishing, Yeovil (2015)